67 Ready-To-Run Programs In BASIC: graphics, home & business, education, games

Acknowledgements

Dianne Wiles-Watson for the artwork

Radio Shack - Thanks to Hy Siegel and Terry Phelps for the loan of the Screen Printer, as well as the entire company for giving us a darned good computer at a reasonable price.

John Watson - Who helped out with many of the business applications programs.

My Family - For tolerating me (most of the time) during this venture.

And finally,
Computer Center of the Central Missouri State University

No. 1195
$12.95

67 Ready-To-Run Programs In BASIC: graphics, home & business, education, games

by Wm. Scott Watson

TAB BOOKS Inc.
BLUE RIDGE SUMMIT, PA. 17214

FIRST EDITION

THIRD PRINTING

Copyright © 1981 by TAB BOOKS Inc.

Printed in the United States of America

Library of Congress Cataloging in Publication Data

Watson, William Scott
     67 ready-to-run programs in BASIC
     Includes index.
     1. Computer programs.   2. Basic (Computer program lan-
guage)   I. Title.
QA76.6.W384   002.64′25   80-28282
ISBN 0-8306-9660-1
ISBN 0-8306-1195-9 (pbk.)

Contents

Introduction

Perhaps the most frustrating chore for the average microcomputer owner is finding an adequate supply of software. For many owners, the only apparent alternative to hiring a professional programmer is to rely on the preprogrammed or "canned" software available from the manufacturer and various mail-order companies. However, with a majority of preprogrammed software costing from two to twenty dollars for simple games and up to one hundred dollars for complex business management packages, it is easy to see why many owners simply cannot *afford* to build a large enough software library to fully utilize the potentials of their computers.

This book will help you build a satisfactory software library at a reasonable cost. Each program uses a low level form of BASIC and is designed to run on 4k of memory or less. Ultimately, the programs in this book should provide the microcomputer owner with many hours of use in various applications, for approximately the average price of a single canned program. You can bring Las Vegas to your home and gamble with the best without ever risking your paycheck, or, if you choose, race out to the far reaches of the galaxy to battle deadly enemies and still return home in time to balance your checkbook.

Wm. Scott Watson

Chapter 1
Book Basics

The programs in this book are arranged in four categories;
- Games,
- Graphics,
- Home and Business Management, and
- Educational.

In order to provide full aid to debugging and modification, each program is supported with full documentation. For each program listing, there is a section of REMARKS. The remarks section will list any specific information needed to use the program that is not mentioned in the program listing.

Also included in each program's documentation is a VARI-ABLE LIST. This list identifies all important variables, as well as their specific function. This section will be particularly useful to users who wish to study, modify, or simply change the level of difficulty of a program.

For users with intermediate programming skills, I have included a section of SUGGESTED VARIATIONS. Although this section is by no means comprehensive, there are enough modifications mentioned to increase the actual number of programs in this book to well over two hundred.

Finally, there is a SAMPLE RUN. If the user has typed a program in correctly, the sample run listed with each program will give a good indication of what to expect. Please take note that because of the lengthy repetition of many of the programs, the sample runs are often not complete. Again, they should give a good indication of what to expect.

These programs should give you hours of practical use and entertainment. Doublecheck each program with the listing to insure that you have not made a typographical error. If all else fails and a program still will not run correctly, relax. Go get a drink of water, take the dog for a walk, and start again from scratch.

Once you have a program "up and running," you will probably want to save it on cassette tape (or whatever storage method you use). Use a good quality cassette, make two copies of each program, and you should not experience any retrieval problems.

Chapter 2
Program Language

All of the programs listed in this book are written using Radio Shack's TRS-80 Level 1 BASIC (*B*eginner's *A*ll-purpose *S*ymbolic *I*nstruction *C*ode). This version of BASIC was chosen because of its universality, as well as the ease in which this low level BASIC may be modified to run on other BASIC speaking computers. This chapter will deal with Level 1 BASIC in detail. Using the Level 1 BASIC guide below, the user can modify the listed programs to run on any of the popular BASICS with relatively little difficulty. If your computer does not use Level 1 BASIC, consult your user's manual to determine what modifications are necessary.

Although the programs in this book are listed using Radio Shack's Level 1 BASIC, the programs are by no means strictly limited to the TRS-80 (Fig. 2-1), Dartmouth BASIC, the father of all BASICS, including Radio Shack's Level 1, is a comprehensively defined computer language. If you were to study the BASICS utilized by various microcomputer brands, you would find that nearly all of the dissimilarities would fall into one of two categories:

■ special commands or statements not included in Dartmouth BASIC, or

■ differences of syntax usage in the various commands and statements.

All of the essential commands and statements used in the programs in this book are consistant with Dartmouth BASIC. Therefore, the

Fig. 2-1. Radio Shack TRS-80 Microcomputer System.

first category of conversion problems has been resolved. The following statement definition guide explicitly defines the syntax usage for commands and statements used in Level 1 BASIC. Therefore, the user, understanding the style of syntax used by their machine (which is usually described by materials supplied with the computer), will be able to adapt the syntax or "convert" the programs in this book for use on *any* BASIC speaking microcomputer on the market.

Only the program statements and intrinsic (library) functions used in the programs in this book are listed below. A complete summary of Level 1 BASIC can be found in Radio Shack's Level 1 BASIC User's Manual.

Statements

PRINT—Prints the value of a variable or whatever is contained within quotes. Example—10 PRINT "GAMES WON= ";A

INPUT—Allows data to be entered from the keyboard. Example—10 INPUT A. A PRINT statement may also be placed within an INPUT. Example—10 INPUT "HOW MANY GAMES DO YOU WISH TO PLAY";A

LET—(optional) Assigns a number to a variable. Example—10 LET A=5.

GOTO—Branches unconditionally to specified line number. Example—10 GOTO 150.

IF-THEN—Conditional test. Example—10 IF A=1 THEN B=B+1

IF-GOTO—Branches to specified line number only if conditional is true. Example—10 IF A=1 GOTO 150

IF-GOSUB—Branches to specified subroutine only if conditional is true. Example—10 IF A=1 GOSUB 150

FOR-NEXT—Performs a multi-statement loop. Example—10 FOR X=1T05 20 NEXT X

STEP—Increments a FOR-NEXT loop. Example—10 FOR X=1T05 STEP 2

END—Ends program execution. Example—10 END

GOSUB—Branches unconditionally to a specified subroutine. Example—10 GOSUB 150

RETURN—Ends subroutine and branches to statement following GOSUB.

ON-GOTO—Multi-statement branch. Example—10 ON X GOTO 10,20,30

ON-GOSUB—Multi-subroutine branch. Example—10 ON X GOSUB 10,20

CLS-Clears screen. Example—10 CLS

SET—Lights up graphic block at specified x,y coordinates. Example—10 SET (10,20)

RESET—Turns off graphic block at specified x,y coordinates. Example—10 RESET (10,20)

POINT—Interrogates graphic point at specified x,y coordinates. Returns a 1 if point is lit, or 0 if point is not lit. Example—10 IF POINT (10,20)=1 GOTO 150

PRINT AT—Begins printing at specified address. Example—10 PRINT AT 100, "100"

PRINT TAB (X)—Begins printing X spaces from left margin. Example—10 PRINT TAB (10); "10"

Intrinsic (Library) Functions

INT(X)—Returns the integer value of X—Example 10 X=INT(X).

ABS(X)—Returns the absolute value of X—Example 10 X=ABS(X).

RND(X)—When X is greater than zero, returns a number between 1 and X. When X equals zero, returns a number between 0 and 1. Example 10 X=RND(5).

Arithmetic Operators

+   Addition
−   Subtraction
*   Multiplication
/   Division
=   Equal to
<>   Not equal to
<=   Less than or equal to
>=   Greater than or equal to
>   Greater than
<   Less than

Logical Operators

+   Or
*   And

Variables

Numeric—Letters A through Z.
String—A$, B$.
Array—A(X).

12

Chapter 3
Program Size

In keeping with the goal of universality, all of the programs in this book have been written to run (either directly or in some cases indirectly) on 4K or less of memory. If a program listing exceeds your computer's memory capacity, the following modifications should be made to the program. First, delete all unnecessary REM or remark statements you might have added to the program. Next, delete all spaces in the program statements that are not vital for syntax. This may make the program difficult to read and debug, but it does free a lot of memory space in many cases. Finally, if the above steps don't help, use abbreviations wherever possible. I have used abbreviations in many of the programs for such repetitive commands such as PRINT and GOTO, and if your computer will support abbreviations, it would be wise to get in the habit of using them.

If your computer will not support abbreviated statements, use the following list to modify the abbreviations in the program listings back to the original statement.
PRINT—P.
END—E.
THEN—T.
GOTO—G.
INPUT—IN.
FOR—F.
NEXT—N.
STEP—S.

TAB—T.
INT—I.
GOSUB—GOS.
RETURN—RET.
ABS—A.
RND—R.
SET—S.
RESET—R.
POINT—P.
PRINT AT—P.A.

Occasionally you might find that if you dress up a program with too many visuals, you will run out of memory quite rapidly. I have attempted to make these programs as eye appealing as feasible. If your computer has the extra memory capacity, don't be afraid to add some fancy graphics.

Chapter 4
Programming Tips,
Inspirations, and Proverbs

You're on thin ice reusing cassettes. Cassettes are cheap. The time you spend retyping a lengthy program due to misalignment of your recorder's erase head isn't.

It may be trite, but its true—a program is never finished. There is always a better way to do what you have done.

If there is a users group in your area, I would recommend that you join it. If there isn't, see if you can't get one started. The amount of information floating around in these groups will make them a profitable experience for any computer owner. If you plan to start one, contact the manager of your local computer outlet. He should be more than willing to help, since an increased awareness of his product will ultimately mean more customers.

If you smoke while you use your computer, be careful that ashes do not fall between the keys. Ashes can cause a nasty keybounce.

Keybounce causes multiple characters to appear on the screen after typing only one key. It can be cured quite easily in most cases. First, remove the cap of the offending key(s). This usually can be done using a strong paper clip bent in the shape of a "J". Next, wipe the key's switch contacts gently with a cotton swab sprayed with a good television tuner cleaner/lubricant. Replace the key's cap and give 'er a try.

It is even easier to prevent keybounce than to cure it. A folded pillowcase makes an excellent keyboard cover.

An experienced programmer once told me: "A program should never run correctly the first time. If it does, there's something wrong that you've missed." Sounds logical to me.

If you store more than one program per cassette side, be sure to leave plenty of space between programs.

It isn't a good idea to copy or otherwise reproduce a copyrighted program except for your own use. Sitting in jail for selling a bootlegged Spacewars program is no way to waste your time.

Avoid using low quality tapes to store your programs on. Many times these cassettes will have dropouts in the ferrous recording material that will not store data properly.

When storing a program on tape, its a good idea to make two copies in case one doesn't record properly or is later damaged.

If you are in danger of power surges or interruptions as you program, make frequent copies as you progress. This will probably make more sense after you have lost a lengthy program due to a power failure.

Know when to stop. If you just can't seem to figure out a problem after an hour or so, work on something else for a while. The answer will probably come to you in the middle of the night.

Always trust hunches when you wake up in the middle of the night.

You really shouldn't discard any work you have done because of a seemingly unsolvable problem.

Even if your practical knowledge of computing is near zilch, chances are that your friends will think you avate garde for owning one.

Repeat after me: "Its only a stupid machine.. Its only a stupid machine...Its only a stupid machine."

Computer technology is a young science. There is no such thing as a computer expert, only men with various degrees of understanding. This is true no matter what the experts tell you.

If it is possible, don't sell your programs, barter them. Not only do both parties profit from a barter, its untaxable!

Strive to understand *all* of your system's capabilities. It is beyond the scope of this book to teach BASIC or programming skills. There are many fine books on the market to pick up where your instruction manual leaves off.

You should plan your program to achieve the desired result using as little memory as possible. This leaves plenty of room for modification and "dressing up" later.

If your computer is situated in a location where static electricity is a problem, try to discharge the static before operating the system. Yes, static can affect even the smallest microcomputer.

Try to store your program cassettes in a cool, dry, dust-free environment. Also, don't place cassettes on or near the power supply. The magnetic field created by the supply can play some nasty tricks on your recordings.

Try to stay up to date with state-of-the-art developments. There is a lot of literature, books, magazines, etc. that can teach you new tricks with your computer.

It is always a good idea to make sure that a mail-order company is reputable before ordering peripherals for your system.

For many users, a shorthand block logic is better than a rigidly structured flowchart. Experiment with both to see which works better for you.

Hitting, threatening, bouncing, shaking, and cussing out a computer will rarely result in cooperation. But, it feels good.

Chapter 5
The Games

For many owners, perhaps the most attractive feature of their microcomputer system is the ability to not only entertain the user with the hundreds of game programs available from the manufacturer and various software dealers, but also allow the owner to "whip up" a few of his own games. Although the computer game is not yet legend, the demand for computer game software certainly points to this in the future.

In the early years of computer development (which, by the way, isn't that long ago), access to computer games was limited only to those crafty programmers and technicians who possessed the secret passwords to the game libraries of university and corporative computer laboratories. Today, the availability of these same game programs is quickly approaching surplus levels. Problem—most owners simply cannot afford the price of a complete library of popular computer games, and of those who can, many find themselves spending hours coding their "bargain buys" into a BASIC that their computer can interpret.

Here, then, are a collection of some of the all-time favorite game programs, along with a few new ones, to try your "luck" on. Some of the programs are easy enough for a child to beat, some are a bit more difficult for the intermediate gamesman, and a few are downright devious.

The programs are grouped according to similarity. In other words, gambling games with gambling games, space games with space games, and so on. There is no reason why you shouldn't skip around in this chapter, if gambling isn't your cup of tea, move on to something more appealing. But, before you file this book away for future reference, try *all* of the programs at least once. There just may be a "sleeper" in here somewhere that you may have passed over.

Above all, don't be afraid to modify these programs to suit your own tastes. You will find that many of the suggested variations in this chapter are devoted to changing the level of difficulty of the game. I strongly urge you to follow these suggestions until you have come up with a game that, to you, is highly playable.

I have seen accountants, students, and housewives bent over a computer terminal keyboard, eyes bloodshot, fingers numb, dripping sweat as they watch a horde of approaching enemy space-craft seal the fate of their fleet. What does any self-respecting starship captain do after his fleet is destroyed by the enemy? Type the word RUN, sit back, and start all over again, of course.

Perhaps this is the most redeeming value of the computer game. It allows the player to escape reality, earthly pressures, and a second notice electric bill with a form of entertainment that, unlike television in my opinion, commands attention through the requirement of the *use* of intelligence. When the video monitor is a window through which the user can truly see a part of himself, then and only then can the program be correctly labled a computer game.

Display plays an important part in computer games, as this is how the player will perceive the output and translate it into something meaningful. When possible, graphics should be used to spice up the output (i.e. an animated example of what has occured).

Although for the most part I have limited graphics within programs to the programs in the Graphics chapter, you will notice that in some programs such as BOMBSQUAD a small section of the program is used to graphically illustrate an important development in the game (in this example, an exploding bomb). If you are running a machine that does not have graphic capabilities, you may wish to eliminate these sections and replace them with alpha-numeric messages such as "KA-BOOM!". If you are running a machine other than a TRS-80, turn forward to the Graphics chapter where the graphics commands and layout are explained so that you can make the necessary modifications for the programs in this chapter.

Well, if you've read everything up to here, you are now ready to dive right in! Good luck and good gaming!

Craps

In this game, the player first places a bet and then rolls a pair of dice. If the first roll totals to 2, 3, or 12, the player automatically loses his bet. If the first roll is a 7 or 11, he automatically wins. If none of the above totals are reached on the first roll, the total is called the "point." The player continues to roll the dice until he again rolls his point and wins his bet, or rolls a 7 or 11 and loses. See Fig. 5-1.

Variable List

B - Amount of money in players account.
C - Amount of player's bet.
Y - Die #1 value.
Z - Die #2 value.
T - First roll total.
U - Subsequent roll totals.

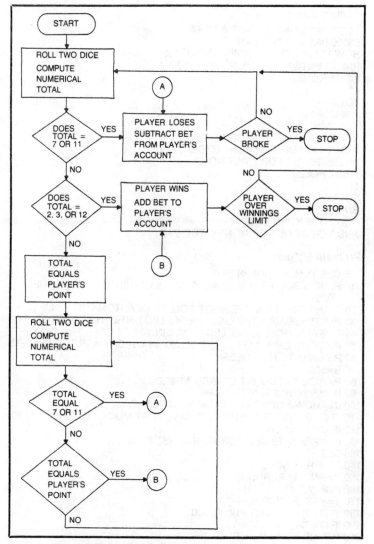

Fig. 5-1. Flowchart for the Craps game.

Suggested Variations

■ Change starting account amount as controlled in line #70.

■ Change amount to break the bank as controlled in line #470.

■ Experiment with loading the dice. Don't worry about credibility, most non-computerists won't trust your computer anyway.

Sample Run

```
YOUR ACCOUNT STANDS AT $500
$5000 BREAKS THE BANK.
HOW MUCH DO YOU WISH TO BET?500
PRESS ENTER FOR YOUR FIRST ROLL?
FIRST ROLL:
4 3
TOTAL—7
A NATURAL!
YOU WIN.
YOUR ACCOUNT STANDS AT $1000
HOW MUCH DO YOU WISH TO BET?1000
PRESS ENTER FOR FIRST ROLL?
FIRST ROLL:
1 1
TOTAL—2
SNAKE EYES!
YOU LOSE YOUR BET.
AND YOU'RE OUT OF MONEY. TOO BAD.
```

Program Listing

```
  5 CLS: P.:P.:P. "CRAPS":P.
 10 P. "IF A PLAYER ROLLS A 2, 3, OR 12 ON HIS FIRST ROLL, HE
    LOSES."
 20 P. "A 7 OR 11 ON THE FIRST ROLL IS AN AUTOMATIC WIN."
 30 P. "OTHERWISE, THE DICE ARE ROLLED UNTIL THE TOTAL OF THE"
 40 P. "FIRST ROLL IS ROLLED AGAIN, IN WHICH CASE THE PLAYER"
 50 P. "WINS, OR A 7 OR 11 IS ROLLED, IN WHICH CASE THE PLAYER"
 60 P. "CRAPS OUT (LOSES)."
 70 B=500
 80 P. "YOUR ACCOUNT STANDS AT $";B
 90 P. "$5000 BREAKS THE BANK"
100 IN. "HOW MUCH DO YOU WISH TO BET";C
110 IF C>B THEN P. "YOU DON'T HAVE THAT MUCH, HOTSHOT": G.80
120 IF C<=O G. 80
130 IN. "PRESS ENTER FOR YOUR FIRST ROLL";A$
135 CLS
140 P. "FIRST ROLL:"
150 Y=RND (6):Z=RND(6)
160 P.:P. Y,Z: P.
170 T=Y+Z: P. "TOTAL-----";T
180 IF (T=2)+(T=3)+(T=12) G. 300
190 IF (T=7)+(T=11)G.400
200 P T;" IS YOUR POINT"
210 IN. "PRESS ENTER FOR YOUR NEXT ROLL";A$:CLS
```

22

```
220 Y=RND(6):Z=RND(6):U=Y+Z
230 P. "ROLL:":P.
240 P. Y;Z:P.
250 P. "TOTAL---";U
260 IF U=T G. 450
270 IF (U=7)+(U=11) G. 350
280 P. "NOT YOUR POINT, KEEP ROLLING THE BONES!"
290 G. 210
300 IF T=2 THEN P. "SNAKE EYES!"
310 IF T=3 THEN P. "COCK EYES!"
320 IF T=12 THEN P. "BOXCARS!"
330 G. 360
350 P. "YOU CRAPPED OUT!"
360 P. "YOU LOSE YOUR BET":B=B-C
370 IF B<=0 G. 600
380 G. 80
400 P. "A NATURAL!"
410 G. 460
450 P. "YES! YOU HIT YOUR POINT."
460 P. "YOU WIN YOUR BET":B=B+C
470 IF B>=5000 G. 620
480 G. 80
600 P. "AND YOU'RE OUT OF MONEY. TOO BAD."
610 END
620 P. "HEY! YOU'VE BROKEN THE BANK WITH $";B
630 END
```

Inn-B-Tween

The computer deals two cards to the player. The player must then bet on the probability of the next card dealt lying numerically between the first two. An ace may count as either 1 or 14.

Variable List

B - Players account amount.
T - Determine which card is being dealt.
F - Value of first card dealt.
S - Value of second card dealt.
C - Amount of players bet.
Q - Value of third card dealt.
A - Used in card dealing routine. Value of A is assigned to either F, S, or Q depending upon which card is being dealt.

Suggested Variations

■ Change starting account amount as defined in line #60.
■ Add a bank breaking amount as used in other gambling games - see *CRAPS*.

■ Cause the player to pay a small amount to the house whenever he passes cards by betting $0.

■ This is a tough one—add a system to allow splits. That is, if a player's first two cards are alike, he can double his bet and play the two cards as two separate hands, each having an additional card dealt to it.

Sample Run

```
PRESS ENTER TO DEAL THE FIRST TWO CARDS?
10
2
YOUR ACCOUNT STANDS AT $1000
HOW MUCH DO YOU BET?1000
2
NO! YOU LOSE!
AND YOU'RE ALL OUT OF MONEY, BRIGHTEYES.
```

Program Listing

```
  5 CLS:P.:P.:P."INN-B-TWEEN":P.
 10 P. "THIS IS A CARD GAME SIMILAR TO ACEY-DEUCEY WITH"
 20 P. "THE EXCEPTION THAT NO SPLITS ARE ALLOWED.THE PLAYER"
 30 P. "IS DEALT TWO CARDS. HE MUST THEN BET ON IF THE NEXT"
 40 P. "CARD DEALT WILL LIE NUMERICALLY BETWEEN THE FIRST
      TWO."
 50 P. "ACES CAN COUNT AS EITHER 1 OR 14"
 60 B=1000
 70 IN. "PRESS ENTER TO CONTINUE";A$:CLS
100 IN.  "PRESS ENTER TO DEAL  THE FIRST  TWO CARDS";A$:
     P.:P.
110 T=O
120 A=RND(14):IF A=1 G. 120
130 IF A>10 G. 160
140 P. A:P.
142 IF T=0 G. 170
145 IF T=1 G. 200
148 G. 300
160 IF A=11 THEN P. "JACK"
162 IF A=12 THEN P. "QUEEN"
164 IF A=13 THEN P. "KING"
168 IF A=14 THEN P. "ACE: IF T 2 GOS. 400
169 G. 142
170 F=A
175 T=T+1: G. 120
200 S=A
210 P. "YOUR ACCOUNT STANDS AT $";B
215 IN. "HOW MUCH DO YOU BET";C
220 IF C>B G. 210
230 IF C>0 THEN 240
232 CLS:P. "NEXT HAND...":G. 100
240 T=T+1: G. 120
300 Q=A
310 IF F<S G. 350
315 IF (Q>S)*(Q<F) THEN 370
320 P. "NO! YOU LOSE!":B=B−C
```

```
325 IF B<=0 G. 1000
330 IN. "PRESS ENTER TO CONTINUE";A$:G. 232
350 IF (Q>F)*(Q<S) THEN 370
360 G. 320
370 P. "HURRAY! YOU WIN $";C:B=B+C
380 IF B>=10000 G. 1100
390 G. 330
400 IN. "DOES YOUR ACE COUNT AS 1 OR 14";A
410 IF (A=1)+(A=14) G. 420
415 P. "ILLEGAL VALUE":G. 400
420 RETURN
1000 P. "AND YOU'RE ALL OUT OF MONEY, BRIGHTEYES."
1010 END
1100 P. "WOW! YOU'VE BROKEN THE BANK WITH $";B
1110 END
```

Dice

Player bets on a number from 1 to 6 representing the spots on each of three dice rolled by the computer. He is repayed his bet matches, or loses his bet if no matches occur.

Variable List

E - Player's account amount.
F - Player's monetary bet.
D - Player's die bet.
A - Value of die #1.
B - Value of die #2.
C - Value of die #3.
R - Die rolled. Value of R is assigned to either A, B, or C depending on which die is being rolled.
X - Time delay loop.

Suggested Variations

■ Maximum bet is $10,000 as controlled in line #80 change it to suit your tastes.

■ Starting account amount is controlled in line #50.

■ Change bank breaking amount as defined in line #321.

■ Allow credit to the player if he loses all of his money. This may be used in any of the gambling games.

Sample Run

```
YOU NOW HAVE $ 10000
WHAT IS YOUR BET ?10000
```

WHAT NUMBER DO YOU WISH TO BET ON (1 TO 6)?5
FOUR
ONE
SIX
HERE IS THE PAYOFF
YOU LOSE YOUR BET ON A NON-MATCH.
AND YOU'VE LOST ALL OF YOUR MONEY.

Program Listing

```
    5 CLS:P.:P.:P. "DICE":P.
   10 P. "IN THIS GAME, YOU PLACE A BET (MAXIMUM $10000), PICK"
   20 P. "A NUMBER FROM 1 TO 6. THE COMPUTER WILL ROLL THREE"
   30 P. "DICE, AND YOU WILL BE PAID ACCORDINGLY.$500000 BREAKS"
   40 P. "THE BANK."
   50 E=10000
   55 P.:P.:IN. "PRESS ENTER TO CONTINUE"A$:CLS
   60 P. "YOU NOW HAVE $";E
   70 IN. "WHAT IS YOUR BET";F
   80 IF F<=10000 G. 90
   83 IF E>=F G. 90
   85 P. "INVALID BET":G. 60
   90 IN. "WHAT NUMBER DO YOU WISH TO BET ON (1 TO 6)";D
  100 FOR N=1 TO 3
  110 R=RND(6)
  120 IF R=1 THEN P. "ONE":G. 150
  125 IF R=2 THEN P. "TWO":G. 150
  130 IF R=3 THEN P. "THREE":G. 150
  135 IF R=4 THEN P. "FOUR":G. 150
  140 IF R=5 THEN P. "FIVE":G. 150
  145 IF R=6 THEN P. "SIX":G. 150
  150 P.:IF N=1 G. 160
  152 IF N=2 G. 170
  155 N. N
  156 G. 180
  160 A=R
  165 G. 155
  170 B=R
  175 G. 155
  180 C=R
  185 P. "HERE IS THE PAYOFF:":FOR X=1TO500:N.X
  210 IF D=A G. 220
  215 G. 230
  220 IF D=B G. 240
  225 G. 260
  230 IF D=B G. 250
  235 G. 270
  240 IF D=C G. 310
  245 G. 300
  250 IF D=C G. 300
  255 G. 290
  260 IF D=C G. 300
  265 G. 290
  270 IF D=C G. 290
  280 P. "YOU LOSE YOUR BET ON A NON-MATCH"
  285 E=E-F:G. 320
```

26

```
290 P. "HOUSE PAYS 1 TO 1 ODDS ON A SINGLE NUMBER MATCH"
295 E=E+F:G. 320
300 P. "HOUSE PAYS 2 TO 1 ODDS ON A DOUBLE NUMBER MATCH!"
305 E=E+(2*F):G. 320
310 P. "HOORAY! HOUSE PAYS 5 TO 1 ODDS ON A TRIPLE NUMBER
    MATCH!!"
315 E=E+(5*F)
320 IF E<=0 G. 325
321 IF E>500000 G. 340
322 G. 55
325 P. "AND YOU'VE LOST ALL OF YOUR MONEY"
327 END
340 P. "GREAT JOB! YOU'VE BROKEN THE BANK WITH $";E
350 END
```

Slot Machine

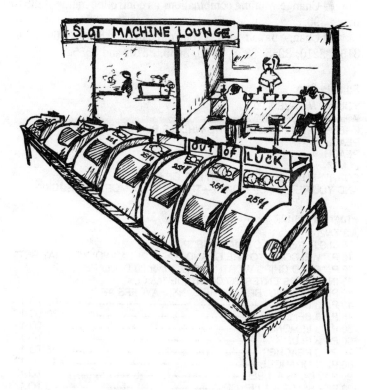

In this souped up reproduction of the old one-armed bandit, the player may bet using gold tokens worth $1, $2, $5, $10, or $20. Payoffs are calculated according to the wheel combination.

Variable List

T - Players account amount.
Z - Time delay loop.
B - Player's bet.
A - Value of wheel #1.
E - Value of wheel #2.
C - Value of wheel #3.
D - Total value of A, E, & C.

Suggested Variations

■ Change starting account amount as defined in line #3.
■ Change amount of tokens allowable as defined in line #158 to line #162.
■ Change winning combinations as controlled in line #335 to line #390.
■ Change payoff odds as controlled in lines 3010, 3060, 3110, 3155, 3210, 3255, 3355, 3410, 3455, 3510, and 3555.

Sample Run

```
YOU NOW HAVE $ 20
WHAT IS YOUR BET? 20
PRESS ENTER TO START THE WHEELS SPINNING!?
PEACH
PEACH
LEMON
SORRY, BUT YOU LOSE YOUR BET OF $ 20
AND YOU'RE OUT OF MONEY—TRY AGAIN TOMORROW, SUCKER!
```

Program Listing

```
  3 T=20
  5 CLS:P.:P.:P. "SLOT MACHINE":P.
 10 P. "WELCOME TO THE GRAND WATSON CASINO! YOU MAY BET"
 20 P. "GOLD CHIPS WORTH 1, 2, 5, 10, or 20 DOLLARS."
 25 IN. "PRESS ENTER TO CONTINUE";A$:CLS
 30 P. "$5000 WILL BREAK THE BANK! PAYOFFS ARE:"
 40 P. "3 BARS-----------------------------------------------------------100 TO 1"
 45 P. "3 BELLS-----------------------------------------------------------80 TO 1"
 50 P. "3 LEMONS --------------------------------------------------------50 TO 1"
 60 P. "3 PLUMS----------------------------------------------------------30 TO 1"
 70 P. "3 PEACHES-------------------------------------------------------25 TO 1"
 80 P. "3 ORANGES ------------------------------------------------------10 TO 1"
 90 P."2 BARS & 1 BELL------------------------------------------------10 TO 1"
100 P."2 BELLS & 1 LEMON -------------------------------------------9 TO 1"
110 P."2 LEMONS & 1 PLUM ------------------------------------------8 TO 1"
120 P."2 PLUMS & 1 PEACH-------------------------------------------7 TO 1"
130 P."2 PEACHES & 1 ORANGE-------------------------------------5 TO 1"
140 P."2 ORANGES & ANYTHING --------------------------------------2 TO 1"
150 IN. "PRESS ENTER TO CONTINUE";A$:CLS
```

```
155 P. "YOU NOW HAVE $";T
156 IN. "WHAT IS YOUR BET";B
158 IF (B=1)+(B=2)+(B=5)+(B=10)+(B=20) THEN 165
160 P. "YOU MAY BET 1, 2, 5, 10, OR 20 DOLLARS ONLY":G. 156
165 IF B<=T G. 170
167 P. "YOU DON'T HAVE THAT MUCH, TURKEY!":G. 155
170 IN. "PRESS ENTER TO START THE WHEELS SPINNING!";A$
175 FOR O=1 TO 3
180 P=0
190 R=RND(6)
191 FOR Z=1TO1000:N. Z
192 IF R=1 THEN P. "BAR":L=300000:G. 300
200 IF R=2 THEN P. "BELL":L=20000:G. 300
205 IF R=3 THEN P. "LEMON":L=3000:G. 300
210 IF R=4 THEN P. "PLUM":L=100:G. 300
215 IF R=5 THEN P. "PEACH":L=20:G. 300
220 IF R=6 THEN P. "ORANGE":L=3
300 P.: IF O=1 G. 500
310 IF O=2 G. 600
320 IF O=3 G. 700
330 N. O
335 IF D=900000 G. 3000
340 IF D=60000 G. 3050
350 IF D=9000 G. 3100
355 IF D=300 G. 3150
360 IF D=60 G. 3200
362 IF D=9 G. 3250
365 IF D=620000 G. 3300
370 IF D=43000 G. 3350
375 IF D=6100 G. 3400
380 IF D=220 G. 3450
385 IF D=43 G. 3500
386 IF D=300006 G. 3550
387 IF D=20006 G. 3550
388 IF D=3006 G. 3550
389 IF D=106 G. 3550
390 IF D=26 G. 3550
400 P. "SORRY, BUT YOU LOSE YOUR BET OF $";B
405 FORZ=1TO1500:N. Z
410 T=T-B: IF T<=0 G. 5000
415 CLS: G. 30
500 A=L
510 G. 330
600 E=L
610 G. 330
700 C=L
710 D=A+E+C
720 G. 330
3000 P. "JACKPOT!!! 100 TO 1 PAYOFFS!!"
3010 T=T+(100*B)
3020 G. 3800
3050 P. "YOU WIN AT 80 TO 1 ODDS"
3060 T=T+(80*B)
3070 G. 3800
3100 P. "YOU WIN AT 50 TO 1 ODDS"
3110 T=T+(50*B)
3120 G. 3800
```

```
3150 P. "YOU WIN AT 30 TO 1 ODDS"
3160 T=T+(30*B)
3170 G. 3800
3200 P. "YOU WIN AT 25 TO 1 ODDS"
3210 T=T+(25*B)
3220 G. 3800
3250 P. "YOU WIN AT 10 TO 1 ODDS"
3260 T=T+(10*B)
3270 G. 3800
3300 G. 3250
3350 P. "YOU WIN AT 9 TO 1 ODDS"
3360 T=T+(9*B)
3370 G. 3800
3400 P. "YOU WIN AT 8 TO 1 ODDS"
3410 T=T+(8*B)
3420 G. 3800
3450 P. "YOU WIN AT 7 TO 1 ODDS"
3460 T=T+(7*B)
3470 G. 3800
3500 P. "YOU WIN AT 5 TO 1 ODDS"
3510 T=T+(5*B)
3520 G. 3800
3550 P. "YOU WIN AT 2 TO 1 ODDS"
3560 T=T+(2*B)
3570 G. 3800
3800 IF T>=5000 G. 4000
3810 G. 155
4000 P. "INCREDIBLE! YOU'VE BROKEN THE BANK! CONGRATULA-
     TIONS!"
4010 END
5000 P. "AND YOU'RE OUT OF MONEY—TRY AGAIN TOMORROW,
     SUCKER!"
5010 END
```

Horse Race

The player bets on the horse of his choice to win. Winning payoffs are calculated from the pre-race pari-mutual odds.

Variable List

H - Player's account amount

Z - Time delay loop

J - Player's monetary bet.

I - Player's horse bet.

A - Horse number 1's position.

B - Horse number 2's position.

C - Horse number 3's position.

D - Horse number 4's position.

E - Horse number 5's position.

F - Horse number 6's position.

G - Horse number 7's position.
L - Decides if Horse #1 advances.
M - Decides if Horse #2 advances.
N - Decides if Horse #3 advances.
O - Decides if Horse #4 advances.
P - Decides if Horse #5 advances.
Q - Decides if Horse #6 advances.
R - Decides if Horse #7 advances.
V - Payoff.

Suggested Variations

■ Design a system to calculate and pay different odds for each horse each race.

■ Design a system to allow a bet of win, place, or show. (Be careful with this one.)

■ Change starting account amount as defined in line #2.

■ Allow more than one player to place a bet and keep each player's account total. Hint: Use array locations to represent each player's account and bets if you run out of letter variables.

■ Design a system to display the player's bets below the "track" as the race is being run.

Sample Run
```
ENTER THE NUMBER OF THE HORSE YOU WISH TO BET ON?5
YOUR ACCOUNT STANDS AT $ 1000
HOW MUCH DO YOU WISH TO BET?1000
YOU HAVE BET $ 1000 ON HORSE #5
IF THIS CORRECT TYPE IN ANY NUMBER EXCEPT 1?2
S.......I.......I.......I.......I.......F
  1
2
  3
4
  5
   6
 7
S.......I.......I.......I.......I.......F
S.......I.......I.......I.......I.......F

       1
            2
    3
        4
  5
        6
          7
S.......I.......I.......I.......I.......F
```

Program Listing

```
    1 P. "****************************************************"
    2 P.: H=1000
    3 P." H O R S E R A C E "
    4 P.
    5 P. "AT THE BEAUTIFUL WATSON DOWNS"
    6 P "****************************************************"
    7 G. 19
   10 IF H<=0 G. 2000
   19 FOR Z=1 TO 1500:N. Z: CLS
   20 P. "HERE ARE THE HORSES RUNNING AND THEIR ODDS:"
   25 P."=============================== = ="
   30 P. "1) GOLDEN MANURE---------------------------------------8:1"
   40 P. "2) MR. GLUE-----------------------------------------------3:1"
   50 P. "3) BEER BELLY --------------------------------------------2:1"
   60 P. "4) PREGNANT GLORY---------------------------------20:1"
   70 P. "5) CRUDFACE----------------------------------------------15:1"
   80 P. "6) UNCLE JOHN'S ITCH-----------------------------------7:1"
   90 P. "7) DUCK WALKER------------------------------------------6:1"
   95 P."=============================== = ="
  100 IN. "ENTER THE NUMBER OF THE HORSE YOU WISH TO BET
      ON"; I
  103 P. "YOUR ACCOUNT STANDS AT $";H
  105 IN. "HOW MUCH DO YOU WISH TO BET";J
  110 IF J<=H G. 120
  112 P. "THAT'S MORE THAN YOU HAVE, JOKER":G. 103
  120 CLS:P. "YOU HAVE BET $;J;" ON HORSE #";I
  125 P. "IF THIS IS CORRECT TYPE IN ANY NUMBER EXCEPT 1";
  126 IN. Z:IF Z=1 G. 100
  127 CLS
  129 A=0:B=0:C=0:D=0:E=0:F=0:G=0
  130 FOR Z=1 TO 5:P."IT'S POST TIME!": FORY=1TO250:N. Y
  135 CLS:FOR Y=1 TO 250:N. Y:N. Z
  150 P."S......I......I......I......I......I......I......I......I......I......F"
  155 P.TAB(A),"1":IF A=50 G. 1000
  160 P.TAB(B),"2":IF B=50 G. 1050
  165 P. TAB(C),"3":IF C=50 G. 1100
  170 P. TAB(D),"4":IF D=50 G. 1150
  180 P.TAB(E),"5":IF E=50 G. 1200
  185 P.TAB(F),"6":IF F=50 G. 1250
  190 P.TAB(G),"7":IF G=50 G. 1300
  195 P."S......I......I......I......I......I......I......I......I......I......F"
  200 L=RND(2):M=RND(2):N=RND(2):O=RND(2):P=RND(2):Q=RND(2):R=
      RND(2)
  201 IF L=1 THEN A=A+1
  202 IF M=1 THEN B=B+1
  203 IF N=1 THEN C=C+1
  204 IF O=1 THEN D=D+1
  205 IF P=1 THEN E=E+1
  206 IF Q=1 THEN F=F+1
  207 IF R=1 THEN G=G+1
  208 CLS
  210 G. 150
 1000 P. "HOORAY! IT'S GOLDEN MANURE AT THE FINISH!"
 1001 IF I<> 1 G. 1025
 1005 V=J*8:H=H+V
```

```
1010 P. "YOU HAVE WON $";V
1013 G. 10
1025 H=H-J:P."YOU LOSE YOUR BET"
1030 G. 10
1050 P. "MR. GLUE BEATS 'EM BY A MILE!"
1051 IF I<>2 G. 1025
1055 V=J*3:H=H+J
1060 G. 1010
1100 P. "IT'S BEER BELLY AT THE TAPE!"
1101 IF I<> 3 G. 1025
1105 V=J*2:H=H+V
1110 G. 1010
1150 P. "IT'S PREGNANT GLORY BY A STRIDE!"
1151 IF I<>4 G. 1025
1155 V=J*20:H=H+V
1160 G. 1010
1200 P. "INCREDIBLE.....CRUDFACE WINS AGAIN!"
1201 IF I<>5 G. 1025
1210 V=J*15:H=H+V
1220 G. 1010
1250 P. "IT COULDN'T BE... IT IS! UNCLE JOHN'S ITCH IS NUMBER 1!"
1251 IF I<>6 G. 1025
1260 V=J*7:H=H+V
1270 G. 1010
1300 P. "THE MIGHTY DUCK WALKER TAKES THE WINNER'S CUP!"
1301 IF I<> 7 G. 1025
1310 V=J*6:H=H+V
1320 G. 1010
2000 P. "YOUR ACCOUNT IS BUSTED AND YOUR CREDIT'S NO GOOD
        HERE."
2005 P. "BEAT IT.....YA BUM."
2010 END
```

Fokul

Pronounce it anyway you want to. Player must run back to his ship before the Fokul (advancing from the opposite direction) gets there first. Player may shoot at the Fokul at anytime.

Variable List

A - Fokul's energy (Fokul dies when A = 0.)
E - Distance from Fokul to ship.
C - Distance from human to ship.
P - Whether shot hits or misses Fokul.
L - Amount of damage done to Fokul from shot.

Suggested Variations

■ Check out the "you lose" message. Can you apply this display to other games?
■ Change advance rates for human and Fokul as controlled in lines 205 and 220 respectively.
■ Change starting distances to ship as defined in line #140.
■ Change Fokul's starting energy as defined in line #140.

Sample Run

THE FOKUL IS 50 STEPS AWAY FROM YOUR SHIP
YOU ARE 40 STEPS FROM YOUR SHIP
ENTER 1 FOR RUN OR 2 FOR SHOOT?1
YOU ARE 38 YARDS FROM SAFETY

THE FOKUL ADVANCES
THE FOKUL IS 47 STEPS AWAY FROM YOUR SHIP
YOU ARE 38 STEPS FORM YOUR SHIP
ENTER 1 FOR RUN OR 2 FOR SHOOT?2
SHOT MISSES... FOKUL ADVANCES
THE FOKUL IS 44 STEPS AWAY FROM YOUR SHIP
YOU ARE 38 STEPS FROM YOU SHIP
ENTER 1 FOR RUN OR 2 FOR SHOOT?2
SHOT STUNNED FOKUL!
THE FOKUL IS 44 STEPS AWAY FROM YOUR SHIP
YOU ARE 36 STEPS FROM YOUR SHIP
ENTER 1 FOR RUN OR 2 FOR SHOOT?

Program Listing

```
  5 CLS:P.:P.:P."FOKUL":P.
 10 A=0:B=0:C=0:D=0:E=0
 20 P. "ON THE PLANET CLAMELON II, YOU HAVE ENCOUNTERED"
 30 P. "A BEAST KNOWN AS THE FOKUL. THIS BEAST CONSIDERS"
 40 P. "HUMAN FLESH A DELICACY. YOU ARE 50 YARDS"
 50 P. "FROM YOUR SHIP (AND SAFETY). EVERY RUNNING STRIDE"
 60 P. "YOU TAKE IS 2 YARDS. THE FOKUL'S STRIDE IS 3 YARDS."
 70 P. "EACH TURN, YOU MAY ADVANCE 1 STRIDE TOWARDS SAFETY,"
 80 P. "OR SHOOT AT THE FOKUL. HOWEVER, YOUR GUN IS MEANT"
 90 P. "FOR A MUCH SMALLER TARGET THAN A FOKUL, AND UNLESS"
100 P. "YOU HIT IT IN A VITAL AREA (SLIM CHANCE), IT WILL"
110 P. "TAKE QUITE A FEW HITS TO KILL IT."
130 P.:IN. "GOOD LUCK...PRESS ENTER TO START GAME";A$:CLS
140 A=700:C=40:E=50
170 P. "THE FOKUL IS ";E;"STEPS AWAY FROM YOUR SHIP"
175 P. "YOU ARE ";C;"STEPS FROM YOUR SHIP"
180 IN. "ENTER 1 FOR RUN OR 2 FOR SHOOT";Q
200 IF Q=2 G. 1000
205 C=C-2
215 IF C<=0 G. 2000
218 P. "THE FOKUL ADVANCES"
220 E=E-3
235 IF E<=0 G. 3000
240 G. 170
1000 P=RND(3)
1005 IF P=1 G. 1010
1006 IF P=2 G. 1050
1007 P. "SHOT MISSES.....FOKUL ADVANCES"
1008 G. 220
1010 L=RND(10)
1012 IF L<=4 G. 1010
1015 P. "SHOT STUNNED FOKUL!!"
1020 A=A-10*L
1025 GOS. 1500
1026 C=C-2
1030 G. 170
1050 P. "SHOT WOUNDED FOKUL...ADVANCES SLOWLY"
1060 L=RND(6):A=A-10*L:E=E-1
1090 GOS. 1500
1100 G. 170
1500 IF A<=0 G. 2000
1510 IF A<=100 THEN P. "FOKUL'S ENERGY IS LOW"
```

35

```
1520 RETURN
1800 IF C<=0 G. 2500
1810 RETURN
2000 P. "AND THE FOKUL IS DEAD! YOU WIN!"
2010 END
2500 P. "YOU'VE REACHED YOUR SHIP FIRST—YOU WIN!"
2510 END
3000 P. "G-U-L-P!! THE FOKUL HAS REACHED YOUR SHIP FIRST."
3050 IN. "PRESS ENTER TO TAKE YOUR LUMPS";A$:CLS
3100 FOR X=1 TO 1000: P. "YOU LOSE";:N. X
3110 END
```

Super Fokul

This time there are two Fokuls, and they're not interested in eating you, only reaching your ship first and destroying it. Beware! In this souped up version of *FOKUL*, the Fokuls even have guns to shoot at *you* with!

Variable List

A - Distance from Fokul 1 to ship.
B - Distance from Fokul 2 to ship.
C - Distance from human to ship.
D - Fokul 1's power.
E - Fokul 2's power.
F - Human's power.
S - Human stunned or not.
P - Advance amount.
K,G - Hit or miss Fokul, amount of damage.
M - Fokul 2 stunned or not.
Q - Fokul 1 stunned or not.
O - Governs Fokul 1's actions.
I, J - Control of Fokul 1's shot.
T - Governs Fokul 2's actions.
V - Fokul 2's advance.
Y - Fokul 1's advance.
U,W - Control of Fokul 2's shot.

Suggusted Variations

■ Change starting power and distances as defined in Line #151.
■ Change energy requirements for advance and shoot.
■ Change range of advance distances.
■ Change damage amounts of being wounded, stunned.

Sample Run

```
-----------------
RANGE CHART
FOKUL 1 HAS 750 ENERGY UNITS REMAINING
FOKUL 2 HAS 750 ENERGY UNITS REMAINING
YOU HAVE 750 ENERGY UNITS REMAINING
#########
FOKUL 1 IS 600 YARDS FROM YOUR SHIP
FOKUL 2 IS 600 YARDS FROM YOUR SHIP
YOU ARE 600 YARDS FROM YOUR SHIP
::::::::::
WHAT IS YOUR CHOICE (1=MOVE 2=SHOOT)?1
FOKUL 1 SHOOTS AND MISSES YOU!
FOKUL 2 ADVANCES 48 YARDS
YOU APPROACH 89 YARDS

-----------
RANGE CHART
FOKUL 1 HAS 650 ENERGY UNITS REMAINING
FOKUL 2 HAS 700 ENERGY UNITS REMAINING
YOU HAVE 700 ENERGY UNITS REMAINING
################
FOKUL 1 IS 600 YARDS FROM YOUR SHIP
FOKUL 2 IS 552 YARDS FROM YOUR SHIP
YOU ARE 511 YARDS FROM YOUR SHIP
::::::::::
WHAT IS YOUR CHOICE (1=MOVE 2=SHOOT)?2
AT WHICH FOKUL (1 OR 2)?2
FOKUL 2 IS HIT AND WOUNDED!
YOU APPROACH 25 YARDS
FOKUL 1 APPROACHES 73 YARDS
FOKUL 2 APPROACHES 25 YARDS
PRESS ENTER TO CONTINUE?
```

Program Listing

```
  5 CLS:P.:P.:P."SUPER FOKUL":P.
 10 P. "IN THIS GAME, THERE ARE TWO DEADLY BEASTS"
 20 P. "(FOKUL 1 AND FOKUL 2) THAT ARE RACING AGAINST"
 30 P. "YOU TO REACH YOUR SPACESHIP. ALL THREE OF YOU"
 40 P. "BEGIN 600 YARDS AWAY FROM THE SHIP. ON EACH TURN"
 50 P. "YOU HAVE TWO OPTIONS TO CHOOSE FROM:"
 60 P.
 70 P. "1) APPROACH SHIP---BECAUSE OF TERRAIN ASPECTS,"
 80 P. "APPROACH DISTANCES WILL VARY."
 90 P. "OR"
100 P. "2) SHOOT AT FOKUL 1 OR 2---IF YOU STUN A FOKUL,IT"
110 P. "WILL BE UNABLE TO TAKE ANY ACTION FOR 1 TURN."
130 P.:S=0
140 P. "USE YOUR ENERGY WISELY AND YOU MIGHT MAKE IT"
151 D=750:E=750:F=750:A=600:B=600:C=600
160 GOTO 9200
170 IN. "PRESS ENTER TO CONTINUE";A$:CLS
175 P.:P."-------------":P. "RANGE CHART":M=0:Q=0
176 P. "FOKUL 1 HAS";D;" ENERGY UNITS REMAINING"
177 P. "FOKUL 2 HAS";E;"ENERGY UNITS REMAINING"
178 P. "YOU HAVE";F;"ENERGY UNITS REMINING"
```

37

```
179 P. "###############"
180 P. "FOKUL1 IS";A;"YARDS FROM YOUR SHIP"
190 P. "FOKUL 2 IS ";B;"YARDS FROM YOUR SHIP"
200 P. "YOU ARE";C;"YARDS FROM YOUR SHIP"
201 IF S<> 1 G. 210
202 P."YOU ARE STUNNED---CANNOT ACT THIS TURN"
203 G. 1000
204 P. ":::::::::::::::::"
210 P. ":::::::::::::::::"
211 IN. "WHAT IS YOUR CHOICE (1=MOVE 2=SHOOT)";U
212 IF U=2 G. 500
215 IF U=1 G. 220
217 P. "ILLEGAL OPTION": G. 210
220 P=RND(100)
223 P. "YOU APPROACH";P;"YARDS"
224 F=F−50: C=C−P
230 IF C<=0 G. 4500
240 G. 1000
500 IN. "AT WHICH FOKUL (1 OR 2)";N
501 IF N=1 G. 550
503 K=RND(2)
505 IF K=1 G. 540
510 G=RND(10)
512 IF G>= G. 530
513 P. "FOKUL 2 IS HIT AND WOUNDED!"
515 E=E−10*G
520 G. 220
530 P. "FOKUL 2 IS HIT AND STUNNED!"
531 E=E−10*G
533 M=1
535 G. 220
540 P. "SHOT MISSES FOKUL 2"
541 F=F−100
545 G. 1000
550 K=RND(2)
552 IF K=1 G. 590
555 G=RND(10)
557 IF G>=5 G. 575
560 P. "FOKUL 1 IS HIT AND WOUNDED!"
565 D=D−10*G
570 G. 220
575 P. "FOKUL 1 IS HIT AND STUNNED!"
577 D=D−10*G
578 Q=1
580 G. 220
590 P. "SHOT MISSES FOKUL 1"
592 F=F−100
1000 S=0:IF Q=1 G. 1005
1001 IF D<=0 G. 2000
1002 G. 1020
1005 P."FOKUL 1 IS STUNNED---CANNOT ACT THIS TURN"
1007 G. 2000
1008 G. 9100
1010 IF (C<100)*(100<A) G. 1100
1020 O=RND(5)
1021 IF O=3 G. 1100
```

```
1030 Y=RND(100)
1031 P. "FOKUL 1 APPROACHES";Y;"YARDS"
1032 A=A-Y
1033 IF A<=0 G. 4000
1035 D=D-50
1036 IF D<=0 G. 9110
1040 G. 2000
1100 I=RND(3)
1110 IF I=2 G. 1200
1120 P. "FOKUL 1 SHOOTS AND MISSES YOU"
1122 D=D-100
1123 G. 2000
1200 J=RND(10)
1210 IF J>= G. 1300
1220 P. "FOKUL 1 SHOOTS AND WOUNDS YOU!"
1225 F=F-10*J
1227 G. 1030
1300 P. "FOKUL 1 SHOOTS AND STUNS YOU!"
1310 F=F-10*J
1320 S=1
1330 G. 1030
2000 IF M=1 G. 2005
2001 IF E<=0 G. 160
2002 G. 2010
2005 P. "FOKUL 2 IS STUNNED—CANNOT ACT THIS TURN"
2007 G. 160
2008 G. 9000
2010 IF (C<150)*(150<B) G. 2100
2020 T=RND(7)
2025 IF T=4 G. 2100
2030 V=RND(100)
2035 E=E-50
2037 IF E<=0 G. 9010
2040 P. "FOKUL 2 APPROACHES";V;"YARDS"
2050 B=B-V
2055 IF B<=0 G. 4000
2060 G. 160
2100 U=RND(3)
2110 IF U=2 G. 2200
2120 P. "FOKUL 2 SHOOTS AND MISSES YOU"
2130 E=E-100
2140 G. 160
2200 W=RND(10)
2210 IF W>=5 G. 2300
2220 P. "FOKUL 2 SHOOTS AND WOUNDS YOU!"
2230 F=F-W
2235 G. 2030
2300 P. "FOKUL 2 SHOOTS AND STUNS YOU !"
2310 F=F-W
2313 S=1
2315 G. 2030
4000 P "*************":P. "THE FOKULS HAVE REACHED YOUR SHIP
     FIRST!"
4005 P. "YOU LOSE"
4010 END
4020 P. "*****************************":P."YOUR LIFE SUPPORT SYSTEM
     IS DEAD!"
```

```
4030 G. 4005
4500 P. "**************************":P."YOU HAVE REACHED YOUR SHIP
     SAFELY!"
4510 P. "YOU WIN!"
4515 END
4520 P. "**************************":P."BOTH FOKULS ARE DEAD!"
4530 G. 4510
9000 IF E<=0 G. 9010
9005 G. 2010
9010 P. "FOKUL 2 HAS DIED!"
9020 IF (E<=0)*(D<=0) G. 4520
9025 G. 160
9100 IF D<=0 G. 9110
9105 G. 1010
9110 P. "FOKUL 1 HAS DIED!"
9120 IF (D<=0)*(E<=0) G. 4520
9130 G. 2000
9200 IF F<=0 G. 4020
9210 G. 170
```

Xyron VI

A satellite is on a collision course with the player's base He must destroy it by firing nuclear force torpedos at it. You will find that using the deflector beam is only a temporary solution.

Variable List

A - Altitude of Xyron VI.

E - Power.

C - Percent of Xyron VI intact.

P - Plus or minus miles.

F - How much of Xyron VI destroyed by a direct hit.

G - Xyron VI deflected how far.

H - Amount of Syron VI's descent.

U,V - Used in drawing graphic explosion.

L,N - Ranges supplied by library computer.

M - "Percent probability" of Xyron VI being at a certain range.

Suggested Variations

■ Change starting number of power units as defined in Line #4.

■ Change energy cost values of shooting, deflecting, etc.

■ Change rate of descent of Xyron VI.

■ Add a system to prevent Xyron VI from descending after X direct hits.

Sample Run

```
------------------------
RANGE----10648 PLUS OR MINUS 59 KM
POWER UNITS REMAINING-----8
100% OF XYRON VI INTACT

)))))))))) ORDERS ((((((((((
ENTER 1 FOR FORCE TORPEDOS, 2 FOR DEFLECT, 3 FOR REPOWER,
OR 4 FOR LIBRARY COMPUTER (CONSUMES 1 POWER UNIT)?4
LIBRARY COMPUTER-----READY
XYRON VI IS AT WHAT RANGE?10648
PLUS OR MINUS HOW MANY KM?59
XYRON VI IS EITHER AT 10707 OR 10589 KM
IF YOU NEED ADDITIONAL INFORMATION, TYPE IN ANY NUMBER
EXCEPT 1 (WILL COST AN ADDITIONAL POWER UNIT)?1
)))))))))) ORDERS ((((((((((
ENTER 1 FOR FORCE TORPEDOS, 2 FOR DEFLECT, 3 FOR REPOWER,
OR 4 FOR LIBRARY COMPUTER (CONSUMES 1 POWER UNIT)?1
AT WHAT RANGE (ENTER AS KM)?10707
MISS---ACTUAL RANGE WAS 10589 KM
XYRON VI DESCENDS....2510 KM
PRESS ENTER TO CONTINUE?
```

Program Listing

```
  4 E=8:A=10000+RND(2000):C=100
  5 CLS:P.:P.:P."XYRON VI":P.
 10 P. "THE SATELITE XYRON VI IS ON A COLLISION COURSE"
 20 P. "WITH THE MARTIAN MOON PHOBOS, WHERE YOU ARE"
 40 P. "STATIONED AS THE COMMANDER OF A RESEARCH BASE."
 50 P.
 60 P. "YOU MUST DESTROY XYRON VI BY MEANS OF NUCLEAR"
 70 P. "FORCE TORPEDOS. YOU CAN ALSO DEFLECT IT TEM-"
 80 P. "PORARILY USING A DEFLECTOR BEAM. EITHER OF"
 85 P. "THESE OPTIONS CONSUMES 1 POWER UNIT. AT ANY"
 90 P. "TIME YOU MAY ALSO REPOWER OR CONSULT THE COMPUTER"
 95 P. "LIBRARY TO ASSESS THE CORRECT DISTANCE TO XYRON VI"
 97 IN. "PRESS ENTER TO BEGIN";A$:CLS
100 CLS: P. "STATUS REPORT"
105 P. "----------------"
110 P=RND(200):I=RND(2): IF I=1 G. 120
115 B=A-P
```

```
117 G. 130
120 B=A+P
130 P. "RANGE-----";A;"PLUS OR MINUS";P;"KM"
140 P. "POWER UNITS REMAINING-------";E
150 P. C;"% OF XYRON VI INTACT"
155 P.:P.
160 P. ")))))))))) O R D E R S ((((((((("
170 P. "ENTER 1 FOR FORCE TORPEDOS, 2 FOR DEFLECT, 3 FOR
    REPOWER,"
171 IN. "OR 4 FOR LIBRARY COMPUTER (CONSUMES 1 POWER UNIT)
    ";D
173 ON D G. 200,300,175,700
175 E=E+4
180 P. "FOUR POWER UNITS GAINED"
190 G. 400
200 IN. "AT WHAT RANGE (ENTER AS KM)";K
210 IF K=B G. 250
220 P. "MISS---ACTUAL RANGE WAS ";B;"KM"
230 E=E-1:IF E<=0 G. 500
240 G. 400
250 F=(RND(100)/15)*10:IF F> C THEN F=C
251 C=C-F
260 P. "DIRECT HIT!! ";F;"% OF XYRON VI DESTROYED"
270 G. 230
300 G=RND(200)*10+1000
310 P. "XYRON VI DEFLECTED";G;"KM"
315 A=A+G
320 G. 230
400 IF C<=0 G. 510
405 P. "XYRON VI DESCENDS.....":FOR Z=1 TO 1000: N. Z
420 H=RND(200)*10+1000:P. H;"KM"
425 IN. "PRESS ENTER TO CONTINUE";A$:CLS
430 A=A-H
450 G. 100
460 CLS:FOR T=1 TO 150:U=RND(127):V=RND(47):SET(U,V):N. T
465 P.AT455, "COLLISION!! PHOBOS DESTROYED IN BLAST"
470 END
500 P. "PHOBOS POWER DEAD! COLLISION IS IMMINENT!"
504 FOR Z=1 TO 1500:N. Z:G. 465
510 P. "####### XYRON VI COMPLETELY DESTROYED! #######
    ##"
520 P. "YOU WIN! HOORAY!"
530 END
700 P. "LIBRARY COMPUTER-------READY"
701 IN. "XYRON VI IS AT WHAT RANGE";Q
702 IN. "PLUS OR MINUS HOW MANY KM";O
704 P.:L=Q+O:N=Q-O
706 P. "XYRON VI IS EITHER AT";L;" OR ";N;"KM"
707 E=E-1: IF E<=0 G. 500
708 P."TYPE A 1 TO RETURN TO COMMAND STATUS, OR A 2 FOR"
710 IN. "ADDITIONAL INFO. (WILL COST AN ADDITIONAL POWER
    UNIT)";H
715 IF H=1 G. 160
716 IF H=2 G. 718
717 CLS:G.708
718 M=RND(100):IF M<=55 G. 718
```

```
720 IF A=L G. 750
721 Z=RND(8): IF Z=4 G. 730
722 P. "COMPUTED PROBABILITY THAT XYRON VI IS AT";N;"KM--";M;
    "%"
723 IN. "PRESS ENTER TO CONTINUE";A$:CLS:G. 707
730 P. "COMPUTED PROBABILITY THAT XYRON VI IS AT ";L;" KM--";M;
    "%"
740 G. 723
750 Z=RND(8): IF Z=4 G. 775
751 P. "COMPUTED PROBABILITY THAT XYRON VI IS AT ";L;" KM--";M;
    "%"
760 G. 723
775 P. "COMPUTED PROBABILITY THAT XYRON VI IS AT ";N;" KM--";M;
    "%"
777 G. 723
```

Moonbase Fallout

Opposing moon bases fight it out by shooting nukes and avoiding nukes shot at them. Death toll is calculated by proximity of impact.

Variable List

A - U.S.A. people.

B - U.S.S.R people.

C - U.S.A. missiles.

D - U.S.A. anti-missiles.

E - U.S.S.R. missiles.

F - U.S.S.R. anti-missiles.

X - Chance of direct hit on U.S.S.R.

T - Distance from U.S.S.R. base missile lands.

P - People killed by U.S.A. missile.

G - Chance of direct hit on U.S.A.

L - Distance from U.S.A. base missile lands.

N - People killed by U.S.S.R. missile.

M - Chance of U.S.S.R. launching anti-missile.

I - Whether U.S.S.R. anti-missile hits or not.

Z - Whether U.S.A. anti-missile hits or not.

Suggested Variations

■ Add more people to each moonbase as controlled by Line #10.

■ Change deaths-per-miles proximity ratio.

■ Add system to produce anti-missiles.

■ Change starting amount of missiles and anti-missiles as controlled in Line #10.

■ Add a birthrate so that X number of people are born each turn. This can make the game very long and interesting.

Sample Run

U.S.A.-------10000 PEOPLE, 20 MISSILES.
U.S.S.R.-----10000 PEOPLE, 20 MISSILES.

U.S.A.---------10 ANTI-MISSILES (UNRENEWABLE)
U.S.S.R.-------10 ANTI-MISSILES (UNRENEWABLE)

WHAT ARE YOUR ORDERS? INPUT 1 FOR LAUNCH OR 2 FOR
    PRODUCE?1
MISSILE LAUNCHED
U.S.S.R. DOES NOT LAUNCH ANTI-MISSILE

MISSILE EXPLODES 59 MILES FROM U.S.S.R. MOONBASE
410 RUSSIANS DIE FROM THE BLAST AND FROM RADIOACTIVE
    FALLOUT
U.S.S.R. LAUNCHES MISSILE
DO YOU WISH TO LAUNCH AN ANTI-MISSILE (1=YES 2=NO)?
ANTI-MISSILE MALFUNCTION, U.S.S.R. MISSILE INTACT
MISSILE LANDS 90 MILES FROM U.S.A. MOONBASE
    100 AMERICANS DIE FROM THE BLAST AND FROM FALLOUT
PRESS ENTER TO CONTINUE?

Program Listing

```
  5 CLS:P:P.:P."MOON BASE FALLOUT":P.
 10 A=10000:B=10000:C=20:D=10:E=20:F=10
 32 P. "A NUCLEAR WAR HAS BROKEN OUT ON THE SURFACE OF
    THE MOON"
 34 P. "BETWEEN MILITARY EXPERIMENT STATIONS OWNED BY THE
    U.S.A."
 36 P. "AND THE U.S.S.R. EACH IS EQUALLY ARMED WITH 10 ANTI-"
 38 P. "MISSILES, AND A STOCK OF 20 NUCLEAR WARHEADS, WHICH
    MAY"
 40 P. "BE RENEWED.DEATH TOLL IS CALCULATED BY PROXIMITY OF"
 42 P. "IMPACT. IT'S A FIGHT TO THE FINISH! EACH TURN, YOU MAY"
 44 P. "EITHER LAUNCH A MISSILE OR PRODUCE 3"
 46 P. "YOU ARE THE COMMANDER OF THE U.S.A. BASE."
 48 IN. "PRESS ENTER TO START GAME";A$:CLS
 50 G. 91
 90 IN. "PRESS ENTER TO CONTINUE";A$:CLS
 91 P. "            ****** S T A T U S   R E P O R T *****"
 95 P. "----------------------------------------------------------------------------------
100 P. "U.S.A-------";A;"PEOPLE, ";C;"MISSILES."
102 P. "U.S.S.R.----";B;"PEOPLE,";E;"MISSILES."
104 P.
106 P. "U.S.A.---------";D;"ANTI-MISSILES (UNRENEWABLE)"
108 P. "U.S.S.R--------";F;"ANTI-MISSILES (UNRENEWABLE)"
110 P. "----------------------------------------------------------------------------------
120 P.
125 IN. "WHAT ARE YOUR ORDERS? ENTER 1 FOR LAUNCH OR 2 FOR
    PRODUCE";V
130 IF (V=1)*(C>0) G. 200
140 C=C+3: P. "THREE MISSILES PRODUCED":G. 500
200 T=RND(100):X=RND(50):IF X=35 G. 4000
```

```
201 C=C-1
202 P. "MISSILE LAUNCHED...":FOR Z=1 TO 500:N. Z: G. 1000
205 P.
210 P. "MISSILE EXPLODES";T;"MILES FROM U.S.S.R. MOONBASE"
220 P=(100-T)*10:IF P>B THEN P=B
230 P.:P; "RUSSIANS DIE FROM THE BLAST AND FROM RADIOACTIVE
    FALLOUT"
235 B=B-P
240 IF B<=0 G. 2500
500 IF E<>1 G. 550
510 P. "U.S.S.R. BASE GOES INTO MISSILE PRODUCTION"
520 E=E+3: G. 90
550 P. "U.S.S.R. LAUNCHES MISSILE": IF D=0 G. 580
551 E=E-1
560 IN. "DO YOU WISH TO LAUNCH AN ANTI-MISSILE (1=YES 2=NO)"
    ;U
570 IF U<>1 G. 580
572 Z=RND(2):IF Z=2 G. 575
573 P. "ANTI-MISSILE DESTROYS U.S.S.R. MISSILE":D=D-1: G. 90
575 P. "ANTI-MISSILE MALFUNCTION, U.S.S.R. MISSILE INTACT"
576 D=D-1
580 L=RND(100):G=RND(50):IF G=35 G. 5000
590 P. "MISSILE LANDS";L;"MILES FROM U.S.A. MOONBASE"
595 N=(100)-L)*10: IF N>A THEN N=A
600 P. N;" AMERICANS DIE FROM THE BLAST AND FROM FALLOUT"
610 A=A-N: IF A<=0 G. 3000
620 G. 90
1000 IF F=0 G. 1020
1010 M=RND(2):PF M=1 G. 1030
1020 P. "U.S.S.R. DOES NOT LAUNCH ANTI-MISSILE"
1021 G. 205
1030 I=RND(2):P. "U.S.S.R. LAUNCHES ANTI-MISSILE":IF I=2 G. 1040
1032 P. "ANTI-MISSILE DOES NOT DESTROY U.S.A. MISSILE"
1033 F=F-1:G. 205
1040 P. "DIRECT HIT ON U.S.A. MISSILE":F=F-1:G. 500
2500 P. "U.S.S.R. MOONBASE IS DEAD! U.S.A. WINS!"
2505 END
3000 P. "U.S.A. MOONBASE IS DEAD! U.S.S.R. WINS!"
3005 END
4000 P. "DIRECT HIT! U.S.S.R. MOONBASE IS WIPED OUT":G. 2500
5000 P. "DIRECT HIT! U.S.A. MOONBASE IS BLOWN TO PIECES!":G.
      3000
```

Critical Fleet

Human has a fleet of 25 ships. Object is to cross 20 parsecs of enemy space. Enemy ships may or may not appear in each quadrant.

Variable List

P - Number of ships in fleet.
A - Current parsec.
B - Chance of parsec A being clear.
C - Enemy fires laser - hit or miss.
D - Human's laser - hit or miss.
L - Number of enemies destroyed.
F - Quadrant of parsec A

Suggested Variations

■ Change number of ships in fleet as controlled in Line #77.
■ Change number of quadrants in a parsec.
■ If your computer is equipped for it, fool around with some graphics.

Sample Run

STATUS REPORT FOR PARSEC 1

QUADRANT1
NUMBER OF SHIPS REMAINING IN FLEET------25
SENSORS INDICATE ENEMY SHIP APPROACHING
ENEMY FIRES LASER...
DIRECT HIT...1 FLEETSHIP DESTROYED
****** ORDERS *****
FNTER 1 FOR APPROACH OR 2 FOR FIRE LASER?1
2 MORE APPROACH COMMAND(S) ARE NECESSARY TO CROSS
    PARSEC 1
ENEMY SHIP SIGHTED---PRESS ENTER FOR STATUS REPORT
                          STATUS REPORT FOR PARSEC 1

QUADRANT 2
NUMBER OF SHIPS REMAINING IN FLEET------24
SENSORS INDICATE ENEMY SHIP APPROACHING
ENEMY FIRES LASER...
DIRECT HIT....1 FLEETSHIP DESTROYED
****** ORDERS ******
ENTER 1 FOR APPROACH OR 2 FOR FIRE LASER?2
LASER FIRED...
DIRECT HIT...ENEMY SHIP DESTROYED
PRESS ENTER TO CONTINUE?

Program Listing

```
 5 CLS:P.:P.:P. "CRITICAL FLEET":P.
10 P. "YOU MUST CROSS 20 PARSECS OF SPACE PROTECTED"
20 P. "BY A COMPUTER LEFT BY A DEAD RACE. DURING BATTLE,"
30 P. "EACH PARSEC WILL TAKE 3 APPROACH COMMANDS TO
    CROSS."
40 P. "ALIEN WARSHIPS MAY OR MAY NOT APPEAR IN ANY GIVEN"
50 P. "PARSEC, BUT WILL ALWAYS APPEAR ONLY AS A SINGLE SHIP."
60 P. "A DIRECT HIT ON AN ENEMY SHIP WILL DESTROY IT, AND"
70 P. "GUARANTEE THE SAFETY OF YOUR FLEET THROUGH THAT
    PARSEC."
75 P. "YOUR FLEET CONSISTS OF 25 SHIPS."
77 P=25
78 L=0
80 FOR A=1 TO 20
90 IN. "PRESS ENTER TO CONTINUE";A$:CLS
92 B=RND(5):IF B<>2 G. 100
95 P. "PARSEC";A;" IS CLEAR. APPROACHING PARSEC";A+1
97 G. 1000
100 P.
120 IN. "ENEMY SHIP SIGHTED—PRESS ENTER FOR STATUS REPORT"
    ;A$
121 CLS
122 P.TAB(10);"STATUS REPORT FOR PARSEC";A
125 P.TAB(10);"-----------------------":P. "QUADRANT";F+1
130 P. "NUMBER OF SHIPS REMAINING IN FLEET----";P
140 P. "SENSORS INDICATE ENEMY SHIP APPROACHING..."
150 P. "ENEMY FIRES LASER..."
151 C=RND(3):IF C<>1 G. 160
152 P. "ENEMY FIRE MISSES"
154 G. 200
160 P. "DIRECT HIT...1 FLEETSHIP DESTROYED"
165 P=P-1: IF P<=0 G. 2000
```

47

```
200 P. "******* ORDERS *******"
210 IN. "ENTER 1 FOR APPROACH OR 2 FOR FIRE LASER";U
220 IF U=1 G. 300
230 P. "LASER FIRED..."
240 D=RND(2):IF D=1 G. 280
250 P. "LASER MISSES ENEMY SHIP"
260 G. 120
280 P. "DIRECT HIT! ENEMY SHIP DESTROYED"
285 L=L+1
290 G. 1000
300 F=F+1
305 IF F=3 G. 350
310 P. 3-F;" MORE APPROACH COMMAND(S) ARE NECESSARY TO
    CROSS PARSEC";A
320 G. 120
350 P. "PARSEC";A;" HAS BEEN CROSSED SUCCESSFULLY"
1000 N. A
1005 G. 3000
2000 P. "YOUR ENTIRE FLEET HAS BEEN DESTROYED DUE TO YOUR"
2010 P. "INCOMPETENT STRATEGY. YOU LOSE!!"
2020 END
3000 P. "HOORAY! YOU'VE CROSSED 20 PARSECS AND YOU STILL"
3010 P. "HAVE";P;" SHIPS REMAINING IN YOUR FLEET."
3020 P. "YOU DESTROYED";L;"ENEMY SHIPS IN THIS GAME!"
3040 END
```

Robot War

Player must destroy a group of enemy robots before the
robots kill the player (simple enough). If anything less than all of
the robots are destroyed each turn, the robots will produce more
robots. This can get intense!

Variable List

P - Power.
T - Number of robots.

D - Number of robots destroyed each turn.

Z - Number of robots produced each turn.

X - Number of hits made by robot's weapons.

Suggested Variations

■ Change starting number of robots as controlled in Line #60.

■ Change value of starting power as controlled in Line #60.

■ Change amount of robots produced each turn as defined in Line #280.

Sample Run

```
POWER-----------1000 UNITS
NUMBER OF ROBOTS TO DESTROY-----500
YOU MAY FIRE YOUR WEAPONS AT THE ROBOTS OR YOU MAY
GAIN 250 UNITS OF POWER
ENTER 1 FOR SHOOT OR 2 FOR WAIT?1
EACH UNIT OF ENERGY WILL KILL 1 ROBOT IF HIT
HOW MANY UNITS OF ENERGY DO YOU WISH TO FIRE?700
   650 IS MAXIMUM CAPACITY THIS TURN
HOW MANY UNITS OF ENERGY DO YOU WISH TO FIRE?650
   82 ROBOTS DESTROYED
SURVIVORS PRODUCE 339 ROBOTS
ROBOTS FIRE THEIR WEAPONS AT YOU...
HITS---------673
MISSES--------84
OH NO! THE ROBOTS HAVE DESTROYED YOUR LIFE SUPPORT!
YOU LOSE
```

Program Listing

```
  5 CLS:P.:P.:P."ROBOT WAR":P.
 10 P. "STRANDED ON THE PLANET CYBORG, YOU ARE"
 20 P. "CONFRONTED BY AN ARMY OF WARRIOR ROBOTS."
 30 P. "YOU MUST KILL ALL OF THE ROBOTS BEFORE THE"
 40 P. "SURVIVORS CAN PRODUCE MORE."
 60 T=500:P=1000
 70 IN. "PRESS ENTER TO CONTINUE";A$:CLS
 80 P. "POWER--------";P;"UNITS."
 85 P. "NUMBER OF ROBOTS TO DESTROY-----";T
 90 P. "YOU MAY FIRE YOUR WEAPONS AT THE ROBOTS OR YOU
     MAY"
100 P. "GAIN 250 UNITS OF POWER"
110 IN. "ENTER 1 FOR SHOOT OR 2 FOR WAIT";W
120 IF W=1 G. 200
130 P=P+250
140 P. "POWER IS INCREASED BY 250 UNITS"
150 G. 280
200 P. "EACH ENERGY UNIT WILL KILL ONE ROBOT IF HIT"
210 IN. "HOW MANY UNITS OF POWER DO YOU WISH TO FIRE";E
220 IF E>P THEN P. "YOU ONLY HAVE";P;"UNITS":G. 210
230 IF E=P THEN P. "THAT WOULD KILL YOU TOO, STUPID!":G. 210
250 IF E>T+150 THEN P. T+150;" IS MAXIMUM CAPACITY THIS TURN"
     :G.210
```

```
260 D=RND(E):IF D>T THEN D=T
262 P=P-E
265 T=T-D
270 P. D; "ROBOTS DESTROYED":IF T<=0 G. 1000
280 Z=RND(T):T=T+Z:P. "SURVIVORS PRODUCE";Z;"ROBOTS"
300 P.:P."ROBOTS FIRE THEIR WEAPONS AT YOU..."
310 X=RND(T):M=T-X
320 P.:P. "HITS----------";X
330 P. "MISSES--------";M
340 P=P-X:IF P<=0 G. 1500
350 G. 70
1000 P. "HURRAY!! YOU'VE DESTROYED ALL OF THE ROBOTS!"
1010 P. "YOU WIN":END
1500 P. "OH NO! THE ROBOTS HAVE DESTROYED YOUR LIFE
     SUPPORT!"
1510 P. "YOU LOSE":END
```

Hyperspace

Human and computer both have a fleet of 20 ships. On each turn, one ship is sent out on attack. Only one shot is allowed per attack, so the player wants to get as close as possible to the enemy fleet before firing his weapons.

Variable List

H - Number of ships in human's fleet.
C - Number of ships in computer's fleet.
A - Distance from attacker to opposing fleet.
P - Shot hits or misses.
D - Controls computer's actions, shoot or approach.
B - Amount of approach.

Suggested Variations

■ Change starting number of ships as defined in Line #10.
■ Change hit odds according to distance.
■ Use your imagination and get carried away with some graphics.

Sample Run

STATUS REPORT
DISTANCE TO ENEMY FLEET---10000
SHIPS REMAINING IN YOUR FLEET---20
SHIPS REMAINING IN ENEMY'S FLEET---20
***** ATTACK SHIP HAS BEEN DISPATCHED *****
ENTER 1 FOR APPROACH OR 2 FOR FIRE WEAPON?1
:::::::: DISTANCE TO ENEMY FLEET-- 5600 :::::::

ENTER 1 FOR APPROACH OR 2 FOR FIRE WEAPON?2
DIRECT HIT--1 ENEMY SHIP DESTROYED
PRESS ENTER TO CONTINUE?
STATUS REPORT
DISTANCE TO ENEMY FLEET-- 10000
SHIPS REMAINING IN YOUR FLEET--20
SHIPS REMAINING IN ENEMY'S FLEET--19
***** ATTACK SHIP HAS BEEN DISPATCHED *****
ENTER 1 FOR APPROACH OR 2 FOR FIRE WEAPON?2
SHOT MISSES--ENEMY RELEASES ATTACK SHIP
PRESS ENTER TO CONTINUE?

Program Listing

```
5 CLS:P.:P.:P."HYPERSPACE":P.
10 H=20:C=20
20 P. "EACH SHIP GETS ONLY ONE SHIP PER ATTACK. ODDS OF"
30 P. "A DIRECT HIT ARE INCREASED BY DECREASING THE
   DISTANCE"
40 P. "FROM THE ATTACKING SHIP TO THE OPPOSING FLEET."
50 IF H=0 G. 1000
60 IF C=0 G. 1100
70 T=1:A=10000
80 IN. "PRESS ENTER TO CONTINUE";A$:CLS:P."STATUS REPORT"
90 P. "DISTANCE TO ENEMY FLEET----";A
100 P. "SHIPS REMAINING IN YOUR FLEET---";H
110 P. "SHIPS REMAINING IN ENEMY FLEET--";C
115 P. "***** ATTACK SHIP HAS BEEN DISPATCHED *****"
120 IN. "ENTER 1 FOR APPROACH OR 2 FOR FIRE WEAPON ";Q
125 IF Q=2 G. 150
130 GOS. 1500
132 IF A<=0 G. 900
133 CLS
135 P. ":::::::::: DISTANCE TO ENEMY FLEET-- ";A;"::::::::::"
137 G. 120
147 G. 200
150 GOS. 2000
152 IF P=1 G. 160
155 P. "DIRECT HIT! ONE ENEMY SHIP DESTROYED"
157 C=C-1:IF C=0 G. 1100
158 G. 50
160 P. "SHOT MISSES-- ENEMY RELEASES ATTACK SHIP..."
200 T=0:A=10000:IF H=0 G. 1000
201 IN. "PRESS ENTER TO CONTINUE";A$:CLS
205 IF A>5000 G. 253
210 IF A>1500 G. 250
220 P. "ENEMY SHIP FIRES FROM DISTANCE OF";A
230 GOS. 2000
235 IF P<>1 G. 240
237 P. "SHOT MISSES EARTH FLEET":G. 70
240 P. "ENEMY SHIP DESTROYS ONE EARTHSHIP":H=H-1
245 IF H=0 G. 1000
247 G. 200
250 D=RND(3):IF D=1 G. 220
253 FOR J=1 TO 250:N. J:CLS
255 P. "ENEMY SHIP APPROACHES TO";
257 GOS. 1500
```

51

```
260 IF A<=0 G. 950
265 P. A;"MILES"
270 G. 205
900 P. "COLLISION!! EARTHSHIP DESTROYED!"
910 H=H-1:G. 200
950 P. "COLLISION! ENEMY SHIP DESTROYED!"
960 C=C-1:G. 50
1000 P. "EARTH FLEET DESTROYED. ENEMY IS VICTOR."
1010 END
1100 P. "ENEMY FLEET DESTROYED!!! YOU WIN"
1110 END
1500 IF A> 5000 G. 1520
1510 IF A>1000 G. 1550
1515 G. 1600
1520 B=RND(50)*100:A=A-B
1530 RETURN
1550 B=RND(20)*100:A=A-B
1560 RETURN
1600 B=RND(1800):A=A-B
1610 RETURN
2000 IF A>5000 G. 2020
2005 IF A>1000 G. 2050
2010 IF A>500 G. 2100
2015 G. 2150
2020 P=RND(2):RETURN
2050 P=RND(3):RETURN
2100 P=RND(3):RETURN
2150 P=RND(4):RETURN
```

Submarine Battle

Computer has four subs, human has one. Human must destroy all of computer subs before computer subs find and destroy his.

Variable List

I, J - Human's sub's coordinates.

A,B - Computer sub #1's coordinates.

C,D - Computer sub #2's coordinates.

E,F - Computer sub #3's coordinates.

G,H - Computer sub #4's coordinates.

R, S - Coordinates fired at by computer subs.

Suggested Variations

■ With a little revamping, you can turn this into the popular "Battleship" type game.

■ Expand the coordinates above 5.

■ Change number of human and computer subs.

■ Design a system to prevent firing at coordinates repeatedly. See program *ACHILLE'S HEEL* to examine the array status system. However, if you use this, you may wish to decrease the number of computer subs.

Sample Run

```
HUMAN SUB HIDDEN AT COORDINATES 1,5
WHAT COORDINATES DO YOU WISH TO FIRE THE TORPEDO INTO?1,1
SONAR INDICATES COORDINATES 1,1 UNOCCUPIED
COMPUTER SUB # 1 FIRES INTO COORDINATES 4 , 2
COMPUTER SUB # 2 FIRES INTO COORDINATES 3, 3
COMPUTER SUB # 3 FIRES INTO COORDINATES 1 , 4
COMPUTER SUB # 4 FIRES INTO COORDINATES 3 , 5
WHAT COORDINATES DO YOU WISH TO FIRE THE TORPEDO INTO?
```

Program Listing

```
  5 CLS:P.:P.:P."SUBMARINE BATTLE":P.
 10 A=0:B=0:C=0:D=0:E=0:F=0:G=0:H=0
 20 P. "COMPUTER CONTROLS FOUR SUBMARINES, YOU CONTROL
    ONE."
 30 P. "FIRE TORPEDOS AT THE COMPUTER SUBS BY ENTERING"
 40 P. "X AND Y COORDINATES RANGING FROM 1 TO 5."
 60 A=RND(5):B=RND(5):C=RND(5):D=RND(5):E=RND(5):F=RND(5)
 63 G=RND(5):H=RND(5)
 65 P. "WHERE DO YOU WISH TO HIDE YOUR SUB--SEPARATE X"
 67 IN. "AND Y COORDINATES WITH A COMMA";I,J
 70 IF (I>=1)*(I<=5)*(J>=1)*(J<=5) G. 80
 73 P. "COORDINATES RANGE FROM 1 TO 5:G. 65
 80 CLS:P. "HUMAN'S SUB HIDDEN AT COORDINATES";I;",";J
 85 P.:P.
100 P. "WHAT COORDINATES DO YOU WISH TO FIRE THE TORPEDO
    INTO";
101 IN. K,L
102 IF (K=A)*(L=B) G. 200
104 IF (K=C)*(L=D) G. 300
106 IF (K=E)*(L=F) G. 400
108 IF (K=G)*(L=H) G. 500
109 FOR Z=1 TO 4:CLS:FOR X=1 TO 250:N. X
110 P. "SONAR INDICATES COORDINATES";K;",";L;"UNOCCUPIED."
111 FOR X=1 TO 250:N. X:N.Z:CLS
120 FOR X=1 TO 4
122 R=RND(5):S=RND(5)
130 IF(X=1)*(A=0) G. 157
131 IF (X=2)*(C=0) G. 157
132 IF (X=3)*(E=0) G. 157
133 IF (X=4)*(G=0) G. 157
150 P. "COMPUTER SUB #";X;"FIRES INTO COORDI/ NATES";R;
    ",";S
155 IF(R=I)*(S=J) G. 600
157 N. X
160 G. 85
200 P. "DIRECT HIT ON COMPUTER SUB #1":A=0:B=0
201 G. 550
300 P. "DIRECT HIT ON COMPUTER SUB #2":C=0:D=0
```

53

```
301 G. 550
400 P. "DIRECT HIT ON COMPUTER SUB #3":E=0:F=0
401 G. 550
500 P. "DIRECT HIT ON COMPUTER SUB #4":G=0:H=0
501 G. 550
550 IF (A=0)*(C=0)*(E=0)*(G=0) G. 700
560 G. 85
600 P. "DIRECT HIT FROM COMPUTER SUB #";X
601 P. "HUMAN'S SUBMARINE DESTROYED":END
700 P. "ALL COMPUTER SHIPS HAVE BEEN DESTROYED!!"
705 P. "YOU ARE A WORTHY CAPTAIN, INDEED!":END
```

Bombsquad

Up to 6 players take turns defusing bombs by cutting one of three wires. Two of the wires will defuse the bomb when cut. The third, a "trip" wire, will cause the bomb to explode when cut.

Variable List

A,F - Number of bombs defused by players 1-6 (in order).
X - Number of players.
G - Player #'s turn.
N - Round number.
Z - Trip wire.

Suggested Variations

■ Change number of wires, number of trip wires.
■ Can you come up with a better looking explosion?
■ Fix program to accomodate more than 6 players.
■ Examine the scoreboard at the end of the program to see how the scores of only the number of participating players are displayed. Can you devise a shorter method of doing this?

Sample Run

```
HOW MANY PLAYERS (UP TO SIX)?1
HOW MANY ROUNDS DO YOU WISH TO PLAY?1
ROUND 1
IT IS NOW PLAYER # 1's TURN
THE WIRES IN YOUR BOMB ARE COLOR CODED:
RED..........WHITE..........GREEN
ENTER THE NUMBER OF THE COLORED WIRE YOU WISH TO CUT
(1=RED 2=WHITE 3=GREEN)?3
WHEW! THE RED WIRE WAS THE TRIP WIRE
                FINAL SCORE
-------------------------------------------------------
PLAYER #1-----1 BOMBS
```

Program Listing

```
   4 A=0:B=0:C=0:D=0:E=0:F=0
   5 CLS:P.:P.:P."BOMBSQUAD":P.
  20 P. "IN DEFUSING A BOMB, YOU MUST SIMPLY CUT ONE OF THE"
  30 P. "POWER WIRES. HOWEVER, THESE BOMBS HAVE WHAT IS
     CALLED A"
  40 P. "'TRIP' WIRE-- THIS WILL DETONATE THE BOMB WHEN CUT."
  45 P.
  50 IN. "HOW MANY PLAYERS (UP TO 6)";X
  60 IF X>6 THEN P. "INVALID NUMBER OF PLAYERS":G. 50
  80 IN. "HOW MANY ROUNDS DO YOU WISH TO PLAY";M
  82 FOR N=1 TO M
  85 FOR G=1 TO X
  90 P.:P. "IT IS NOW PLAYER #";G;"'S TURN"
 100 P. "THE WIRES IN YOUR BOMB ARE COLOR-CODED:"
 110 P. "RED.........WHITE.........GREEN"
 115 P. "ENTER THE NUMBER OF THE COLORED WIRE YOU WISH TO
     CUT"
 117 IN. "(1=RED 2=WHITE 3=GREEN)";O
 121 IF (O=1)*(O=2)*(O=3) G. 130
 125 P. "INVALID WIRE NUMBER":G. 100
 130 Z=RND(3)
 132 IF O=Z G. 300
 134 IF Z=1 THEN P. "WHEW! THE RED WIRE WAS THE TRIP WIRE"
 136 IF Z=2 THEN P. "WHEW! THE WHITE WIRE WAS THE TRIP WIRE"
 138 IF Z=3 THEN P. "WHEW! THE GREEN WIRE WAS THE TRIP WIRE"
 140 IF G=1 THEN A=A+1
 150 IF G=2 THEN B=B+1
 160 IF G=3 THEN C=C+1
 170 IF G=4 THEN D=D+1
 180 IF G=5 THEN E=E+1
 190 IF G=6 THEN F=F+1
 250 G. 310
 300 CLS:FORU=1 TO 100:R=RND(127):W=RND(47):SET(R,W):N. U
 302 P.AT469, "KA-BOOM! YOU CUT THE TRIP WIRE!"
 303 FOR Z=1 TO 1000:N. Z:CLS
 310 IN. "PRESS ENTER TO CONTINUE";A$:CLS
 311 N. G
 312 N. N
 330 P.                  "F I N A L   S C O R E"
 335 P. "--------------------------------------------------------------------------------"
 350 P. "PLAYER #-----";A;"BOMBS"
 360 IF X>1 G. 370
 365 G. 500
 370 P. "PLAYER #2-----";B;"BOMBS"
 375 IF X>2 G. 380
 377 G. 500
 380 P. "PLAYER#3-----";C;"BOMBS"
 385 IF X>3 G. 390
 387 G. 500
 390 P. "PLAYER #4-----";D;"BOMBS"
 395 IF X>4 G. 400
 397 G. 500
 400 P. "PLAYER #5-----";E;"BOMBS"
 405 IF X>5 G. 410
 407 G. 500
```

410 P. "PLAYER #6-----";F;"BOMBS"
500 END

Knockout

Player must use two dice, either separately or combined, to remove the numbers 1-12 from the playing table.

Variable List

A(I) - Has number been removed from table or not.
A - Value of Die #1.
B - Value of Die #2.
C - Combined value of both dice.
P - Used to see if any numbers remain on table. If P=0 then table is empty.

Suggested Variations

■ Reduce the numbers on the table. Many versions have the numbers 1-9 on the table.

■ Allow a single die to be used to remove more than one number. Example - one of the dice is a five. The number 5 the numbers 2 and 3 or the numbers 4 and 1 could be removed.

Sample Run

DICE ARE: 6 AND 5
YOUR TABLE LOOKS LIKE THIS:
1 2 3 4 5 6 7 8 9 10 11 12
WHAT NUMBER DO YOU WISH TO KNOCK OUT?6
DICE ARE: 5
YOUR TABLE LOOKS LIKE THIS:
1 2 3 4 5 7 8 9 10 11 12
WHAT NUMBER DO YOU WISH TO KNOCK OUT?5
DICE ARE: 6 AND 2
YOUR TABLE LOOKS LIKE THIS:
1 2 3 4 7 8 9 10 11 12
WHAT NUMBER DO YOU WISH TO KNOCK OUT?8

Program Listing

```
 5 CLS:P.:P.:P."KNOCKOUT":P.
10 P. "IN THE GAME OF KNOCKOUT, YOU ROLL TWO DICE EACH
     TURN."
20 P. "THE DICE MAY BE USED SEPARATELY TO REMOVE THEIR RES-"
30 P. "PECTIVE NUMBERS FROM A TABLE OF NUMBERS 1-12, OR THEY"
40 P. "MAY BE ADDED TOGETHER TO REMOVE ONE NUMBER. IF YOU
     DON'T"
50 P. "HAVE A MOVE, ENTER A NEGATIVE NUMBER. YOU WIN IF YOU"
60 P. "CAN KNOCKOUT ALL OF THE NUMBERS 1-12. YOU LOSE IF AT"
70 P. "ANY TIME YOU CANNOT USE AT LEAST ONE OF THE DICE."
```

```
 80 P.:IN. "PRESS ENTER TO START GAME";A$:CLS
100 FOR I=1 TO 12:A(I)=1:N. I
110 A=RND(6):B=RND(6)
120 P. "DICE ARE: ";
122 IF A=0 G. 128
124 P. A;
126 IF B=0 THEN P. "": G. 130
128 P. B
130 P. "YOUR TABLE LOOKS LIKE THIS:"
140 FOR I=1 TO 12
145 IF A(I)=0 G. 160
150 P. I;" ";
160 N. I
170 P.:P.:P.
190 IN. "WHAT NUMBER DO YOU WISH TO KNOCK OUT";G
192 IF G<0 G. 500
195 CLS
200 C=A+B:IF (G=A)+(G=B)+(G=C) G. 210
205 P. "YOUR ONLY POSSIBILITIES ARE";A;",";B;", OR";C
210 IF A(G)<> 0 G. 250
215 P. G;" HAS ALREADY BEEN KNOCKED OUT":G. 190
250 A(G)=0
260 IF G=A THEN A=0:G.275
270 IF G=B THEN B=0
273 IF G=C THEN A=0:B=0 G. 300
275 IF (B=0)+(A=0) G. 300
277 G. 120
300 P=0
310 FOR I=1 TO 12
320 IF A(I)>0 THEN P=P+1
330 N. I
340 IF P=0 G. 350
345 CLS: G. 110
350 P. "K N O C K O U T ! YOU WIN!!!"
360 END
500 REM *** CHECK TO SEE IF PLAYER HAS A MOVE
510 FOR I=1 TO 12
515 IF A(I)>0 G. 530
520 N. I
525 G. 540
530 IF(I=A)+(I=B)+(I=A+B) THEN P. "YOU DO TOO HAVE A MOVE":G.
    190
535 G. 520
540 IF (A=0)+(B=0) G. 300
550 P. "YOU ARE UNABLE TO USE EITHER OF THE DICE"
560 P. "YOU LOSE"
570 END
```

23 Matches

Player and computer take turns removing 1, 2, or 3 matches from a pile. The player forced to take the last match loses. See Fig. 5-2.

THERE ARE 23 MATCHES LEFT
HOW MANY DO YOU TAKE AWAY (1, 2, OR 3)?3_

I REMOVE 1 MATCHES-

THERE ARE 23 MATCHES LEFT

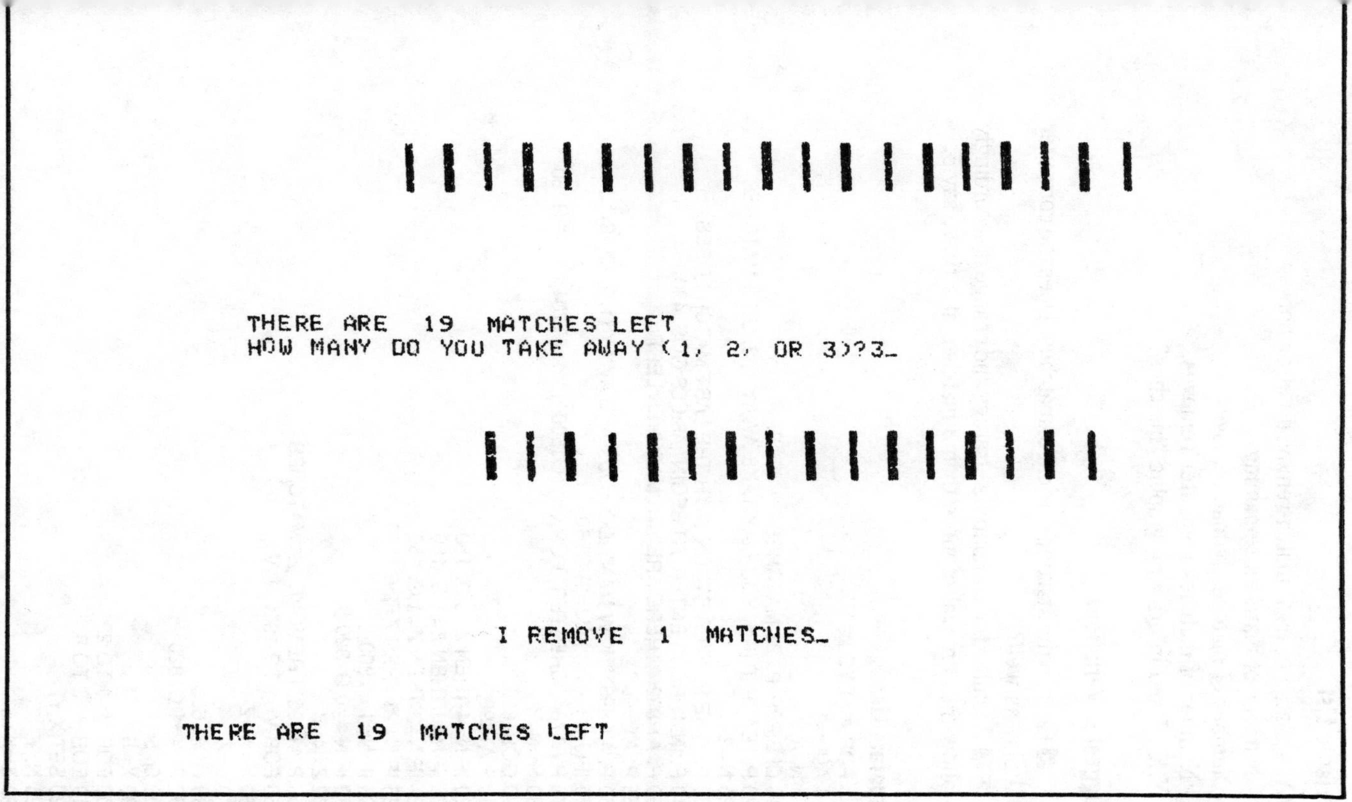

THERE ARE 19 MATCHES LEFT
HOW MANY DO YOU TAKE AWAY(1, 2, OR 3)?3_

I REMOVE 1 MATCHES_

THERE ARE 19 MATCHES LEFT

Fig. 5-2. Example of the 23 Matches game.

Variable List

A(A) - Status of each match-removed yet or not.

N - Number of matches remaining.

J - Number of matches human removes.

Z - Number of matches computer removes.

U,Y,X - Used in drawing graphic "matches".

Suggested Variations

■ Change the starting amount of matches. Does the computer still play as well?

■ Examine the computer's strategy and change it accordingly to allow the removal of more than 3 matches at a time, say 5.

Program Listing

```
  3 FOR A=1 TO 23
  4 A(A)=1
  5 N. A
 10 CLS:P.:P.:P."23 MATCHES GAME":P.
 20 P. "EACH TURN, YOU MAY TAKE AWAY 1, 2, OR 3 MATCHES."
 25 N=23
 30 P. "THE PLAYER STUCK WITH THE LAST MATCH LOSES."
 40 P.:IN. "PRESS ENTER TO BEGIN";A$:CLS:GOS. 490
 50 P. AT 832, "THERE ARE";N; "MATCHES LEFT"
 55 P. AT 596,"
 60 P. AT 896, "HOW MANY DO YOU TAKE AWAY (1, 2, OR 3)";:IN.J
 70 IF(J=1)+(J=2)+(J=3) G. 80
 75 P.AT704,"CHEATER":FORX=1TO1500:N.X:P.AT704,"    ":G. 60
 80 N=N−J
 90 GOS. 600
110 P.AT896,"
120 IF N=4 THEN Z=3:G. 150
122 IF N=3 THEN Z=1:G. 150
124 IF N=2 THEN Z=1:G. 150
126 IF N=23 THEN Z=2:G. 150
128 IF N=1 G. 800
130 IF N<=0 G. 820
132 Z=4−J
150 P.AT596,"I REMOVE";Z;"MATCHES"
155 FOR V=1 TO 1000:N. V
160 N=N−Z
170 J=Z
180 GOS. 600
190 IF N=1 G. 820
200 G. 50
490 X=5
500 FOR U=1 TO 23
510 FOR Y=3 TO 8
520 SET(X,Y)
525 N. Y
530 X=X+5
```

```
540 N. U
550 H=RND(2):IF H=1 G. 50
555 G. 120
560 RET.
600 FOR Z=1 TO J
605 X=5
610 G=1 TO 23
615 IF A(G)=0 G. 650
620 FOR Y=3 TO 8:RESET(X,Y):N. Y
622 A(G)=0
625 G. 690
650 X=X+5:N. G
690 N. Z
700 RETURN
800 P.AT704,"HEY WISE GUY, BET YOU CAN'T BEAT ME AGAIN!!"
810 END
820 P.AT704, "HA HA! YOU JUST GOT BEAT BY A STUPID MACHINE!!"
830 END
```

Russian Roulette For Two

Here's a classic "game" for two players. All the players have to do is enter a number to seed the random number generator. One of the important rules of this game observed throughout the centuries is that the loser must walk the dog. Still got an itchy trigger finger?

Variable List

A$ - Player 1's name.
B$ - Player 2's name.
A - Number of safe turns completed.
E - Whether gun fires or not.
G - Loop to seed random number generator.

Suggested Variations

■ Change the chances of the gun going off by modifying the RND statement in Line #1000

■ This is an excellant program to dress up with some real flashy graphics. Try to keep it prime time, though.

Sample Run

```
WHAT IS THE FIRST PLAYER'S NAME?SCOTT
WHAT IS THE SECOND PLAYER'S NAME?WATSON
SCOTT'S TURN
SCOTT, ENTER A NUMBER FROM 1 TO 100?25
CLICK.....
WATSON'S TURN
WATSON, ENTER A NUMBER FROM 1 TO 100?2
```

KAPOW!
AFTER 1 TURNS, WATSON HAS FINALLY BLOWN HIS/HER
HEAD OFF! SCOTT WINS!

Program Listing

```
  10 CLS:P.:P.:P."RUSSIAN ROULETTE FOR TWO":P.
  20 IN. "WHAT IS THE FIRST PLAYER'S NAME";A$
  30 IN. "WHAT IS THE SECOND PLAYER'S NAME";B$
  40 A=0:B=0
  50 P. A$;" 'S TURN"
  60 P. A$;", ENTER A NUMBER FROM 1 TO 100";:IN. C
  70 FOR D=1 TO C
  75 GOS. 1000
  80 N. D
  90 IF E=3 G. 1518
 100 P.:P.:P.:P."CLICK..."
 110 A=A+1
 120 P. B$" 'S TURN"
 130 P. B$;", ENTER A NUMBER FROM 1 TO 100";:IN.F
 140 FOR G=1 TO F
 150 GOS. 1000
 160 N. G
 170 IF E=3 G. 1600
 180 P.:P.:P.:P."CLICK....."
 190 G. 50
1000 E=RND(6)
1010 RETURN
1500 FOR T=1 TO 8:FOR U=1 TO 250:N. U
1510 P. "KAPOW!":FOR U=1 TO 250:N. U:CLS:N. T
1512 RETURN
1518 GOS. 1500
1520 P. "AFTER";A;"TURNS,"A$;" HAS FINALLY BLOWN HIS/HER"
1530 P. "HEAD OFF! ";B$;"WINS!"
1540 END
1600 GOS. 1500
1610 P. "AFTER";A;" TURNS,";B$;"HAS FINALLY BLOWN HIS/HER"
1620 P. "HEAD OFF! ";A$;"WINS!"
1630 END
```

The Labyrinth

Same basic plot as *FOKUL* except that this time you are in a
dark maze, unarmed. In the classic story of King Minos' labyrinth,
the hero was given a ball of string to unwind as he was led into the
maze so that he could find his way out easily. You don't have any
such luck, though.

Variable List

A - Number of steps away from the Minotaur.
B - Number of steps away from the maze's opening.
E - Safe passage direction each turn.

Suggested Variations

■ Change the starting distances from the player to the opening.

■ Change the starting distances from the player to the Minotaur. Both 1) and 2) are controlled in Line #100.

Sample Run

```
--------------------
THE OPENING (AND YOUR FREEDOM) IS 25 STEPS AWAY
THE MINOTAUR IS 25 STEPS BEHIND YOU!
--------------------
ENTER THE DIRECTION YOU WISH TO FOLLOW BY ENTERING
1 FOR NORTH, 2 FOR EAST, OR 3 FOR WEST?3
NOT A DEADEND--- MOVE ACCEPTED
PRESS ENTER TO CONTINUE?
--------------------
THE OPENING (AND YOUR FREEDOM) IS 24 STEPS AWAY
THE MINOTAUR IS 25 STEPS BEHIND YOU!
--------------------
ENTER THE DIRECTION YOU WISH TO FOLLOW BY ENTERING
1 FOR NORTH, 2 FOR EAST, OR 3 FOR WEST?3
DEAD END---NOW MINOTAUR MOVES
PRESS ENTER TO CONTINUE?
--------------------
THE OPENING (AND YOUR FREEDOM) IS 24 STEPS AWAY
THE MINOTAUR IS 24 STEPS BEHIND YOU!
--------------------
```

Program Listing

```
  2 E=RND(3)
  5 CLS:P.:P.:P."THE LABYRINTH":P.
 10 P. "YOU ARE THE PRISONER OF KING MINOS ON THE ISLAND OF"
 20 P. "CRETE. HE HAS SENTENCED YOU TO BE PLACED IN HIS"
 30 P. "MAZE---THE LABYRINTH BUILT BY THE SCIENTIST DAEDALUS."
 40 P. "EACH TURN YOU WILL HAVE THE OPPORTUNITY TO MOVE
       THROUGH"
 50 P. "THE MAZE---BUT BEWARE, THE DEADLY HALF-MAN/HALF-BULL"
 60 P. "BEAST CALLED THE MINOTAUR IS CLOSE ON YOUR TAIL..."
 70 P.:P."AND IT'S HUNGRY!!":P.
100 A=25:B=25
110 IN. "PRESS ENTER TO CONTINUE";A$:CLS
114 P. "--------------------"
115 P. "THE OPENING (AND YOUR FREEDOM) IS";B;"STEPS AWAY"
120 P. "THE MINOTAUR IS";A;"STEPS BEHIND YOU!"
125 P. "--------------------"
130 P. "ENTER THE DIRECTION YOU WISH TO FOLLOW BY ENTERING"
135 IN. "1 FOR NORTH, 2 FOR EAST, OR 3 FOR WEST";Z
137 IF (Z=1)+(Z=2)+(Z=3) G. 140
138 P. "INVALID DIRECTION---TRY AGAIN":G. 130
140 IF Z=E G. 200
150 P. "DEAD END---NOW MINOTAUR MOVES"
160 G. 250
200 B=B-1:IF B<=0 G. 500
```

```
203 P. "NOT A DEADEND---MOVE ACCEPTED"
204 E=RND(3)
205 G. 110
250 A=A-1:IF A<=0 G. 550
255 IF A<=5 THEN P. "HEY! IT'S RIGHT BEHIND YOU !!"
260 G. 110
500 FOR G=1 TO 5:CLS:FOR R=1 TO 250:N. R
505 P. "HOORAY! HOORAY! YOU'VE MADE IT!! HOORAY! HOORAY!"
510 FOR T=1 TO 250:N. T:N. G
520 END
550 FOR G=1 TO 5:CLS:FOR T=1 TO 250:N. T
555 P.                         " O H N O O O O O O O O O!"
560 FOR E=1 TO 250:N. E:N. G
570 P.:P."THE MINOTAUR HAS EATEN YOU!":P.
580 G. 520
```

Minefield

Player must trudge through a heavily armed minefield. Hitting a mine kills the player and ends the game.

Variable List

S - Number of steps taken safely.
D - Position of mine each turn.
T,X,Y - Used in depicting graphic explosion.

Suggested Variations

■ Change number of steps needed to cross minefield as controlled in Line #140

■ Add a system of Life Units. Hitting a mine subtracts a random number of Life Units. When the L. Us. are depleted, the player dies.

■ Add an enemy chasing the player—many possibilities to this one.

Sample Run

```
YOU HAVE MADE 0 STEPS SAFELY
ONLY 12 STEPS TO GO!
ENTER THE DIRECTION YOU WISH TO GO
1=FORWARD, 2=RIGHT, AND 3=LEFT ?3
WHEW! NO MINE THERE.
PRESS ENTER TO CONTINUE?
YOU HAVE MADE 1 STEPS SAFELY
ONLY 11 STEPS TO GO!
ENTER THE DIRECTION YOU WISH TO GO
1=FORWARD, 2=RIGHT, AND 3=LEFT?2
```

WHEW! NO MINE THERE.
PRESS ENTER TO CONTINUE?

Program Listing

```
  1 S=0
  5 CLS:P.:P.:P."MINEFIELD":P.
 10 P. "YOU MAY MOVE FORWARD, RIGHT, OR LEFT EACH TURN"
 20 P. "AS YOU TRY TO MOVE SAFELY THROUGH A HEAVILY"
 30 P. "ARMED MINEFIELD. YOUR CHANCES OF MAKING IT"
 40 P. "ARE SERIOUSLY LOW--IT WILL TAKE 12 STEPS TO"
 50 P. "CROSS THROUGH THE MINEFIELD. GOOD LUCK!"
 60 P.:P.:P.
 70 IN. "PRESS ENTER TO CONTINUE";A$:CLS
 80 P. "YOU HAVE MADE";S;"STEPS SAFELY"
 85 P. "ONLY";12-S;"STEPS TO GO!"
 90 P. "ENTER THE DIRECTION YOU WISH TO GO"
100 IN. "1=FORWARD, 2=RIGHT, AND 3=LEFT";D
110 IF (D=1)+(D=2)+(D=3) G. 120
115 P. "INVALID DIRECTION":G. 90
120 M=RND(3)
125 IF M=D G. 200
130 P. "WHEW! NO MINE THERE.":S=S-1
140 IF S=12 G. 300
150 G. 70
200 CLS
205 FOR T=1 TO 275
210 X=RND(127):Y=RND(47)
220 SET(X,Y)
230 N. T
235 CLS
240 P.AT470,"))))  KA-BOOM!(((("
242 END
300 FOR K=1 TO 100
305 P. "UNBELIEVABLE.....TREMENDOUS.....FANTASTIC.....SUPER";
310 P. ".....GREAT JOB.....BULLY.....HOORAY.....WHOOPEE.....";
315 N. K
320 P.
325 P. "YOU'VE MADE THROUGH SAFELY, MY FRIEND. BET YOU"
330 P. "CAN'T DO IT AGAIN!"
340 END
```

Sniper

This strategy game can prove to be quite difficult. The object
is to kill the sniper without having any innocent bystanders killed.
You'll be amazed by how this short program can appear to make the
sniper seem almost intelligent!

Variable List

B - Number of bullets sniper has.

P - Number of people sniper has killed.

K,Z,E - Sniper's actions--shoot or wait.

X - Whether sniper's shot hits or misses.

O - Whether sniper is under cover or not.

Y - Whether human's bullet kills sniper or not.

Suggested Variations

■ Change the strategy of the sniper. Let him shoot more than 1 bullet into the crowd at a time.

■ Actually, the sniper begins with 20 bullets. You can change this by modifying the value of B in Line #60.

Sample Run

```
WHAT IS YOUR MOVE? (1=SHOOT 2=WAIT)?1
SNIPER IS UNDER COVER. SHOT MISSES
SNIPER OPENS FIRE!
AN INNOCENT BYSTANDER HAS BEEN SHOT!
PRESS ENTER TO CONTINUE?
WHAT IS YOUR MOVE? (1=SHOOT 2=WAIT)?1
SNIPER IS UNDER COVER. SHOT MISSES
SNIPER OPENS FIRE!
AN INNOCENT BYSTANDER HAS BEEN SHOT!
PRESS ENTER TO CONTINUE?
WHAT IS YOUR MOVE (1=SHOOT 2=WAIT)?1
SNIPER WAS IN OPEN...BUT SHOT MISSED HIM
SNIPER WAITS
PRESS ENTER TO CONTINUE?
WHAT IS YOUR MOVE? (1=SHOOT 2=WAIT)?1
YOU'VE KILLED THE SNIPER!
THE SNIPER KILLED 2 PEOPLE.
```

Program Listing

```
  5 CLS:P.:P.:P."SNIPER":P.
 10 P. "SNIPER HAS THREE CLIPS OF SIX BULLETS EACH."
 20 P. "YOUR MISSION: CAPTURE HIM: DEAD OR ALIVE."
 30 P. "YOU HAVE UNLIMITED AMMO, HOWEVER, A SHOT AT"
 40 P. "HIM WILL ALMOST ALWAYS WARRANT RECIPROCITY."
 60 B=20:P=0
 65 P. "YOU HAVE TWO CHOICES EACH TURN--SHOOT OR WAIT"
 66 IN. "PRESS ENTER TO START GAME";A$:CLS:G. 71
 70 IN. "PRESS ENTER TO START GAME";A$:CLS
 71 IN. "WHAT IS YOUR MOVE? (1=SHOOT 2=WAIT)";A
 90 IF A=1 G. 200
 95 E=RND(3):IF E=2 G. 120
100 P. "SNIPER WAITS..."
110 G. 70
120 P. "SNIPER OPENS FIRE!"
125 X=RND(2):IF X=1 G. 140
130 P. "AN INNOCENT BYSTANDER HAS BEEN SHOT!"
132 P=P+1:B=B-1:IF B=0 G. 1000
134 IF P=10 G. 2000
```

```
135 G. 70
140 P. "WHEW! SHOT MISSES THE CROWD."
142 B=B–1:IF B=0 G. 1000
150 G. 70
200 O=RND(2):IF O=1 G. 210
202 P. "SNIPER IS UNDER COVER... SHOT MISSES"
203 Z=RND(2):IF Z=1 G. 120
205 G. 100
210 Y=RND(6):IF Y=4 G. 250
215 P. "SNIPER WAS IN OPEN.. BUT SHOT MISSED HIM."
220 K=RND(2):IF K=1 G. 120
230 G. 100
250 P. "YOU'VE KILLED THE SNIPER!"
252 P. "THE SNIPER KILLED";P;"PEOPLE."
255 END
1000 FOR Z=1 TO 1000:N.Z:P. "THE SNIPER HAS RUN OUT OF AMMO!"
1010 P. "HE SURRENDERS PEACEFULLY!"
1020 G. 252
2000 P. "HEY! THE SNIPER HAS 10 INNOCENT BYSTANDERS"
2010 P. "DUE TO YOUR INCOMPETENCE. YOU ARE BEING RELIEVED!"
2020 END
```

Target Zero

Player fires missiles at enemy fortresses. One of the five fortresses is a nuclear missile site. When hit, the game ends. Otherwise the game ends at 20 misses. Note: this program allows a cheater to fire at non-existant targets like Target #100 or Target #1.5. You may wish to correct this.

Variable List

A - Number of hits.
B - Number of misses.
C - Position of nuclear site each turn.
E - Whether shot hits or misses.
I - Whether shot at nuclear site hits or misses.

Suggested Variations

■ Add or subtract number of misses that ends game as defined in Line #160

■ Change number of targets.

■ Change number of nuclear sites.

Sample Run

```
HITS----------0
MISSES-------- 0
YOU HAVE YOUR CHOICE OF 5 TARGETS
ENTER YOUR TARGET NUMBER (1-5)?2
DIRECT HIT!
PRESS ENTER TO CONTINUE?
HITS----------- 1
MISSES-------- 0
YOU HAVE YOUR CHOICE OF 5 TARGETS
ENTER YOUR TARGET NUMBER (1-5)?3
DIRECT HIT!
PRESS ENTER TO CONTINUE?
HITS----------- 2
MISSES-------- 0
YOU HAVE YOUR CHOICE OF 5 TARGETS
ENTER YOUR TARGET NUMBER (1-5)?5
MISS--WAS NOT THE NUKE SITE
HITS----------- 2
MISSES-------- 1
YOU HAVE YOUR CHOICE OF 5 TARGETS
ENTER YOUR TARGET NUMBER (1-5)?
```

Program Listing

```
 5 CLS:P.:P.:P."TARGET ZERO":P.
10 A=0:B=0
20 P. "AS THE OPERATOR OF A LARGE CANNON"
30 P. "YOU HAVE YOUR CHOICE OF 5 TARGETS"
```

68

```
40 P. "TO SHOOT AT. HOWEVER, ONE OF THESE"
50 P. "TARGETS IS AN ENEMY NUCLEAR MISSLE"
60 P. "SITE - A DIRECT HIT WILL RESULT IN"
70 P. "YOUR DESTRUCTION. THE GAME ENDS AT"
80 P. "20 MISSES."
90 C=RND(5)
95 IN. "PRESS ENTER TO CONTINUE";A$:CLS
96 P. "HITS---------";A
97 P. "MISSES-------";B
100 P. "YOU HAVE YOUR CHOICE OF 5 TARGETS."
110 IN. "ENTER YOUR TARGET NUMBER (1-5)";D
120 IF D=C G. 300
130 E=RND(2):IF E=1 G. 150
132 P. "DIRECT HIT!":A=A+1
135 G. 90
150 P. "MISS—WAS NOT THE NUCLEAR SITE"
160 B=B+1:IF B=20 G. 200
170 G. 90
200 CLS:P.:P."YOU HIT";A;"TARGETS BEFORE ACCUMULATING"
210 P. "20 MISSES"
220 END
300 CLS
301 FOR Y=1 TO 6:FOR N=1 TO 250:N. N
302 P.. "OH NO! THAT'S THE NUCLEAR SITE!"
303 FOR N=1 TO 250:N.N:CLS:N.Y
305 I=RND(3):IF I=2 G. 320
310 P. "KA-BOOM! YOU'VE BEEN BLOWN TO PIECES!"
315 END
320 P.:P..P."WHEW! YOUR SHOT MISSED THE NUKE SITE!
325 G. 160
```

Deathrace

If you think this is morbid, you should see the graphic version down at your local pinball joint. Some people may not appreciate this program. Then again, some people don't appreciate a good "blood and guts" movie.

Variable List

A—Human's speed.

B—Computer's speed.

C—Human's ammo.

D—Computer's ammo.

F—Number of spectators killed by human's weapon.

U—Amount of computer's ammo destroyed by human.

P—Computer car's action.

G—Number of bullets fired at spectators by computer.

H—Number of spectators killed by computer's weapon.

I—Amount of human's ammo destroyed by computer.

Suggested Variations

■ Tone it down a bit when your grandma visits.

■ Change end of race speed as controlled in Line #'s 165 and 250.

■ Change amount of ammo at start.

■ Change amount of ammo gained at pitstop.

Sample Run

```
CURRENT RACE STANDINGS
DRIVER                    SPEED         BULLETS
HUMAN                       0            500
COMPUTER                    0            500
ENTER 1 FOR PITSTOP, 2 FOR FIRE GUNS AT SPECTATORS,
OR 3 FOR FIRE GUNS AT COMPUTER CAR.?2
HOW MANY SHOTS DO YOU WISH TO FIRE?250
100 AT A TIME IS THE MAXIMUM
RESULTS OF 100 BULLETS FIRED:
15 SPECTATORS KILLED
SPEED IS INCREASED TO 15 MPH
********************
COMPUTER CAR MOVES INTO ACTION
********************
COMPUTER CAR OPENS FIRE ON YOU—DESTROYS 294 ROUNDS
OF YOUR AMMUNITION
PRESS ENTER TO CONTINUE?
CURRENT RACE STANDINGS
DRIVER                    SPEED         BULLETS
HUMAN                      15            106
COMPUTER                    0            450
ENTER 1 FOR PITSTOP, 2 FOR FIRE GUNS AT SPECTATORS,
OR 3 FOR FIRE GUNS AT COMPUTER CAR.?
```

Program Listing

```
  5 CLS:P.:P.:P."DEATHRACE":P.
 10 A=0:B=0:C=500:D=500
 20 P. "YOU ARE IN A RACE. A RACE THAT MEASURES"
 30 P. "VEHICLE ACCELERATION AS 1 M.P.H. FOR EACH"
 40 P. "SPECTATOR THE DRIVER KILLS. THE RACE ENDS AT"
 50 P."300 M.P.H. BOTH YOU AND YOUR OPPONENT, A CAR
 55 P. "CONTROLLED BY A COMPUTER, BEGIN WITH 500"
 60 P. "BULLETS. A PITSTOP WILL RELOAD YOUR GUNS"
 70 P. "WITH 100 BULLETS."
 75 IN. "PRESS ENTER TO BEGIN RACE ";A$:CLS
 80 P. "CURRENT RACE STANDINGS"
 90 P. "DRIVER            SPEED          BULLETS"
100 P. "HUMAN               ";A;"           ";C
110 P. "COMPUTER            ";B;"           ";D
120 P.:IF C <> 0 G. 130
125 P. "YOU ARE OUT OF AMMO, A PITSTOP IS MANDATORY"
127 C=C+100:G. 200
130 P. "ENTER 1 FOR PITSTOP, 2 FOR FIRE GUNS AT SPECTATORS"
```

```
132 IN. "OR 3 FOR FIRE GUNS AT COMPUTER CAR.";R
135 IF R=2 G. 140
136 IF R=3 G. 170
137 G. 127
140 IN. "HOW MANY SHOTS DO YOU WISH TO FIRE ";E
142 IF E>C THEN P. "YOU ONLY HAVE ";C;" BULLETS!":G. 140
143 IF E> 100 THEN P. "100 AT A TIME IS MAXIMUM":E= 100
145 C=C−E
150 P. "RESULTS OF ";E;" BULLETS FIRED:":F=RND(E)
155 P. F;" SPECTATORS KILLED"
160 A=A+F:P. "SPEED IS INCREASED TO ";A;" M.P.H."
165 IF A>=300 G. 500
167 G. 200
170 IF C<50 THEN P. "NOT ENOUGH AMMO TO DO SO":G. 130
171 P. "YOU FIRE 50 BULLETS"
172 U=RND(D):D=D−U
174 P. "YOU HAVE DESTROYED ";U;" ROUNDS OF THE COMPUTER
    CAR'S"
175 P. "AMMUNITION"
200 P.:P. "*********************"
205 P.     "COMPUTER CAR MOVES INTO ACTION"
207 P.     "*********************"
210 IF D<=20 THEN 270
220 P=RND(3):IF P=2 G. 300
230 G=RND(D):ID D>100 THEN G=100
232 D=D−G
235 P. "COMPUTER CAR FIRES ";G;" BULLETS WITH THE FOLLOWING
    RESULTS"
240 H=RND(G):P. H;" SPECTATORS KILLED":B=B+H
250 IF B>=300 G. 600
260 IN. "PRESS ENTER TO CONTINUE ";A$:CLS:G. 80
270 P. "COMPUTER CAR DECIDES TO PITSTOP":D=D+100
280 G. 260
300 IF D< 50 G. 230
305 D=D−50:I=RND(C):C=C−I
310 P. "COMPUTER CAR OPENS FIRE ON YOU—DESTROYS ";I;
    " ROUNDS"
320 P. "OF YOUR AMMUNITION"
330 G. 260
500 P. "YOU HAVE EXCEEDED 300 M.P.H. BY ";A−300;"!"
510 P. "YOU WIN!"
520 END
600 P. "COMPUTER CAR EXCEEDS 300 M.P.H. BY ";B−300;"!"
610 P. "YOU LOSE"
620 END
```

Chicken!

Yes, this is the legendary game we all heard of as kids, only now you can play it without chancing dad's car. However, your ego might get damaged after a few rounds of trying to second guess the computer.

Variable List

H—Number of points awarded to human.
C—Number of points awarded to computer.
R—Number of rounds in a match.
P—Lane human's car is in.
E—Lane computer's car is in.

Suggested Variations

■ Change odds of computer car changing lanes as controlled in Line #250.

■ Expand number of lanes and add computer cars.

■ This is a great chance to add some fancy graphics and impress your friends.

Sample Run

HOW MANY ROUNDS DO YOU WISH TO PLAY?1
BOTH CARS START IN LANE 1
CARS ARE 100 YDS. APART
CARS ARE 50 YDS. APART
CARS ARE 15 YDS. APART
ENTER 1 FOR STAY IN LANE 1 OR 2 FOR CHANGE TO LANE 2?2
COMPUTER CAR CHANGES TO LANE 2
COLLISION—LANE 2. COMPUTER IS AWARDED 2 POINTS.
FINAL SCORE AFTER 1 ROUNDS
****

HUMAN------------- 0 POINTS
COMPUTER---------- 2 POINTS

Program Listing

```
 10 CLS:P.:P.:P."CHICKEN!":P.
 20 P. "YOU ARE ABOUT TO PLAY A GAME OF CHICKEN"
 25 P. "AGAINST THE COMPUTER. EACH CAR TRAVELS"
 30 P. "ON A TWO LANE HIGHWAY TOWARDS THE OTHER."
 40 P. "YOU MAY CHANGE LANES OR STAY IN"
 50 P. "LANE 1. POINTS ARE SCORED AS FOLLOWS:"
 60 P. "PASS SAFELY LANE 1-------------HUMAN---------3 POINTS"
 70 P. "PASS SAFELY LANE 2-------------HUMAN---------2 POINTS"
 80 P. "COLLISION LANE 1----------------COMPUTER------3 POINTS"
 90 P. "COLLISION LANE 2----------------COMPUTER------2 POINTS"
100 H=0:C=0
110 IN. "HOW MANY ROUNDS DO YOU WISH TO PLAY ";R
120 FOR X=1 TO R:P. "ROUND #";X
125 IN. "PRESS ENTER TO CONTINUE ";A$:CLS
130 P. "BOTH CARS START IN LANE 1"
140 P.:P.:FOR T=1 TO 1000: N. T
150 P. "CARS ARE 100 YARDS APART"
160 P. :FOR T=1 TO 500: N. T
170 P. "CARS ARE 50 YARDS APART"
180 P.:FOR T=1 TO 500: N. T
190 P. "CARS ARE 15 YARDS APART"
200 IN. ENTER 1 FOR STAY IN LANE 1 OR 2 FOR CHANGE TO LANE 2";
    V
205 IF (V=1)+(V=2) G. 220
207 P. "ILLEGAL LANE":G. 200
220 IF V=2 G. 240
230 P=1
235 G. 250
240 P=2
250 E=RND(2):IF E=2 G. 260
252 P. "COMPUTER CAR STAYS IN LANE 1"
255 G. 300
260 P. "COMPUTER CAR CHANGES TO LANE 2"
265 G. 350
```

```
300 IF P=E G. 325
305 P. "SAFE PASS--LANE 2--HUMAN IS AWARDED 2 POINTS"
310 H=H+2:G. 1000
325 P. "COLLISION--LANE 1--COMPUTER IS AWARDED 3 POINTS
330 C=C+3:G. 1000
350 IF P=E G. 375
355 P. "SAFE PASS--LANE 1--HUMAN IS AWARDED 3 POINTS"
360 H=H+3:G. 1000
375 P. "COLLISION--LANE 2--COMPUTER IS AWARDED 2 POINTS"
380 C=C+2
1000 N. X
1010 P. "FINAL SCORE AFTER ";X-1;" ROUNDS:"
1020 P. "********************************"
1030 P.
1040 P. "HUMAN------------ ";H;" POINTS"
1050 P. "COMPUTER--------- ";C;" POINTS"
1060 P.:END
```

Point of No Return

Player and computer take turns approaching the edge of the world. The player who gets the closest without going over wins the round.

Variable List

H—Number of rounds won by human.
C—Number of rounds won by computer.
R—Number of rounds to be played.
N—Round number.
A—Distance from human to edge.
B—Distance from computer to edge.
G—Advance distance.
T—Controls computer's actions.

Suggested Variations

■ Change starting distance to the edge as defined in Line #120.

■ Change approach maximums as controlled in Line #'s 1000, 1050, and 1100

■ Fix program to accomodate more than 1 human player.

Sample Run

```
ROUND #1
*****************************************
YOU ARE 100 FEET FROM THE EDGE
*****************************************

ENTER 1, 2, OR 3 FOR THE ADVANCE YOU WANT, OR 5 FOR STOP?1
YOU ADVANCE 30 FEET.
*****************************************
YOU ARE 70 FEET FROM THE EDGE
*****************************************

ENTER 1, 2, OR 3 FOR THE ADVANCE YOU WANT, OR 5 FOR
STOP?1
YOU ADVANCE 50 FEET.
*****************************************
YOU ARE 20 FEET FROM THE EDGE
*****************************************

ENTER 1, 2, OR 3 FOR THE ADVANCE YOU WANT, OR 5 FOR
STOP?2
YOU ADVANCE 18 FEET.
*****************************************
YOU ARE 2 FEET FROM THE EDGE
*****************************************

ENTER 1, 2, OR 3 FOR THE ADVANCE YOU WANT, OR 5 FOR
STOP?5
HMMMMM, 2 FEET. LET'S SEE IF I CAN BEAT THAT...
COMPUTER ADVANCES 31 FEET...
        IS NOW 69 FEET FROM THE EDGE.
```

COMPUTER ADVANCES 50 FEET...
          IS NOW 19 FEET FROM THE EDGE.
COMPUTER ADVANCES 14 FEET...
          IS NOW 5 FEET FROM THE EDGE.
COMPUTER ADVANCES 10 FEET...
          IS NOW– 10 FEET FROM THE EDGE.
YAAAAAH! I'M OVER THE EDGE!
FINAL SCORE
COMPUTER---- 0 ROUNDS
HUMAN------- 1 ROUNDS

Program Listing

```
  5 CLS:P.:P.:P."POINT OF NO RETURN":P.
 10 P. "IN THIS GAME, YOU ARE TRYING TO GET CLOSER TO"
 20 P. "THE EDGE OF THE WORLD THAN THE COMPUTER."
 25 H=0:C=0
 30 P. "BOTH START 100 FEET AWAY. ON EACH TURN, YOU HAVE"
 40 P. "YOUR CHOICE OF THREE ADVANCES:"
 50 P. "1) LONG-- MOVES YOU FROM 0 TO 50 FEET."
 60 P. "2) MEDIUM-- MOVES YOU FROM 0 to 25 FEET."
 70 P. "3) SHORT-- MOVES YOU FROM 0 TO 15 FEET."
 90 IN. "HOW MANY ROUNDS DO YOU WISH TO PLAY ";R
100 FOR N=1 TO R
110 IN. "PRESS ENTER TO CONTINUE ";A$:CLS
120 A=100:B=100
130 P. "ROUND #";N
145 P. "*********************************"
150 P. "YOU ARE ";A;" FEET FROM THE EDGE"
155 P. "*********************************"
160 P. "ENTER 1, 2, OR 3 FOR THE ADVANCE YOU WANT, OR 5 FOR"
170 IN. "STOP";D
180 IF D=5 G. 500
190 IF D=1 GOS. 1000
200 IF D=2 GOS. 1050
210 IF D=3 GOS. 1100
220 A=A–G:IF A<=0 G. 900
230 P. "YOU ADVANCE ";G;" FEET"
240 P.:P.:G. 145
500 P. "HMMMMMM, ";A;" FEET. LET'S SEE IF I CAN BEAT THAT..."
510 IF B>50 THEN T=1:G. 540
520 IF B>25 THEN T=2:G. 540
530 IF B>A THEN T=3:G. 550
540 IF B<A G. 800
545 IF B=A G. 850
550 IF T=1 GOS. 100
560 IF T=2 GOS. 1050
570 IF T=3 GOS. 1100
580 B=B–G:P. "COMPUTER ADVANCES ";G;" FEET...":FOR X=1TO500:
    N.X
585 P.TAB(10);"IS NOW ";B;" FEET FROM THE EDGE."
590 IF B<=0 G. 700
600 G. 510
700 P. "YAAAAAAH!! I'M OVER THE EDGE!":H=H+1
710 G. 950
800 P. "HEY! ";B;" FEET IS CLOSER THAN ";A;"! I WIN THIS ROUND!"
```

```
810 C=C+1:G. 950
850 P. "WELL, LOOKS LIKE THIS ROUND IS A DRAW."
860 H=H+1:C=C+1
870 G. 950
900 P. "OVER THE EDGE--YOU AUTOMATICALLY FORFEIT THIS ROUND.
910 C=C+1
950 N. N
960 P. "FINAL SCORE"
970 P. "COMPUTER---- ";C;" ROUNDS"
980 P. "HUMAN------- ";H;" ROUNDS"
990 END
1000 G=RND(50)
1010 RET.
1050 G=RND(25)
1060 RET.
1100 G=RND(15)
1110 RET.
```

Fortune Teller

This one's pretty simple, yet it effectively shows how random number generators can be used for situations other than "hit or miss". All you have to do is press ENTER and everything is taken care of.

Variable List

A—Displays proper Lovelife message.

B—Displays proper Financial message.

C—Displays proper Job Report message.

D—Displays proper Unexpected message.

E—Displays proper Physical message.

F—Displays proper Mental message.

Suggested Variations

■ This one has many possibilities—change it so that the messages fit the categories people are most interested in. Keep it clean, Jack—you've got an image to protect as an intellectual computerist type.

■ Add hoopla like "What is your astrological sign", or "What is your religion".

Sample Run

```
LOVE LIFE REPORT FOR TODAY:
LOVELIFE WILL BE NEUTRAL TODAY
PRESS ENTER TO CONTINUE?
FINANCIAL REPORT FOR TODAY:
YOU'D BETTER STAY AWAY FROM BARGAINS TODAY
PRESS ENTER TO CONTINUE?
JOB REPORT FOR TODAY:
UH OH... TROUBLE AHEAD!
PRESS ENTER TO CONTINUE?
UNEXPECTED EVENTS REPORT:
NO UNEXPECTED EVENTS ARE CLEARLY INDICATED TODAY
PRESS ENTER TO CONTINUE?
PHYSICAL SHAPE REPORT:
LOOK OUT FOR INJURIES TODAY
PRESS ENTER TO CONTINUE?
MENTAL REPORT FOR TODAY:
A SLUGGISH ATTITUDE IS INDICATED
PRESS ENTER TO CONTINUE?
************************************************************
MADAME COMPUTER NEVER LIES!
************************************************************
```

Program Listing

```
 5 CLS:P.:P.:P."FORTUNE TELLER":P.
10 P.:P. "MADAME COMPUTER TELLS ALL..."
20 IN. "WHAT IS THE DATE TODAY ";A$
25 IN. "WHAT IS YOUR BIRTHDATE ";B$
30 A=RND(4):B=RND(4):C=RND(3):D=RND(2):E=RND(3):F=RND(3)
40 P. "LOVE LIFE REPORT FOR TODAY:"
50 IF A<>1 G. 55
52 P. "GOOD LOVE POTENTIAL FOR TODAY!"
```

```
 53 G. 100
 55 IF A<>2 G. 60
 57 P. "ARGUMENTS WITH LOVED ONES ARE INDICATED"
 58 G. 100
 60 IF A<>3 G. 65
 62 P. "SOMEONE NEW WILL ENTER THE SCENE..."
 64 G. 100
 65 P. "LOVELIFE WILL BE NEUTRAL TODAY"
 100 GOS. 1000
 102 P. "FINANCIAL REPORT FOR TODAY:"
 105 IF B<>1 G. 110
 107 P. "GOOD DAY FOR NEW VENTURES!"
 108 G. 200
 110 IF B<>2 G. 115
 112 P. "DON'T GAMBLE TODAY, JACK!"
 113 G. 200
 115 IF B <> 3 G. 120
 117 P. "FINANCIAL POTENTIAL IS NEUTRAL TODAY"
 118 G. 200
 120 P. "YOU'D BETTER STAY AWAY FROM 'BARGAINS' TODAY"
 200 GOS. 1000
 205 P. "JOB REPORT FOR TODAY"
 206 IF C <> 1 G. 210
 207 P. "UH OH!.... TROUBLE AHEAD!"
 208 G. 300
 210 IF C <> 2 G. 215
 212 P. "NEW IDEAS WILL BE YOURS TO CREATE"
 213 G. 300
 215 P. "JOB WILL BE NEUTRAL TODAY"
 300 GOS. 1000
 301 P. "UNEXPECTED EVENTS REPORT"
 305 IF D <> 1 G. 310
 307 P. "SOMETHING UNEXPECTED IS INDICATED TODAY"
 308 G. 400
 310 P. "NO UNEXPECTED EVENTS ARE CLEARLY INDICATED
     TODAY"
 400 GOS. 1000
 402 P. "PHYSICAL SHAPE REPORT"
 405 IF E <> 1 G. 410
 407 P. "PHYSICAL SHAPE LOOKS GOOD TODAY"
 408 G. 500
 410 IF E <> 2 G. 415
 412 P. "LOOK OUT FOR INJURIES TODAY"
 413 G. 500
 415 P. "NOTHING UNUSUAL IS INDICATED"
 500 GOS. 1000
 502 P. "MENTAL REPORT FOR TODAY"
 505 IF F <> 1 G. 510
 507 P. "MENTAL SHAPE LOOKS GOOD TODAY"
 508 G. 600
 510 IF F <> 2 G. 515
 512 P. "A SLUGGISH ATTITUDE IS INDICATED"
 513 G. 600
 515 P. "MENTAL SHAPE IS NEUTRAL FOR TODAY"
 600 GOS. 1000
 602 P. "*************************************************************"
```

```
605 P. "M A D A M E  C O M P U T E R  N E V E R  L I E S !"
606 P. "****************************************************************"
610 END
1000 IN. "PRESS ENTER TO CONTINUE ";A$:CLS
1010 RETURN
```

Guess My Number

Player guesses computer's randomly selected number by use of three question:

█ Is it greater than X (X is a number entered by the player),

█ Is it less than X, or

█ Is it equal to X. Player must guess the number in 10 turns or less.

Variable List

T—Number of guesses made.

X—Computer's number.

Y—Number entered by player to compare with X depending on which question is asked.

Suggested Variations

█ Change range of computer's number as controlled in Line #65.

█ Change number of guesses allowed as controlled in Line #550.

Sample Run

```
THE CHOICES ARE:
1) X> Y
2) X< Y
3) X=Y
THIS IS GUESS # 1
ENTER THE NUMBER OF THE QUESTION YOU WISH TO ASK?1
IS X GREATER THAN WHAT NUMBER?100
---------- YES ----------
THE CHOICES ARE:
1) X>Y
2) X<Y
3) X=Y
THIS GUESS # 2
ENTER THE NUMBER OF THE QUESTION YOU WISH TO ASK?3
IS X EQUAL TO WHAT NUMBER?157
YES!--YOU HAVE WON WITH 8 GUESSES LEFT!
```

Program Listing

```
1 CLS:P.:P.:P."GUESS MY NUMBER":P.
5 T=0
```

```
10 P. "I PICK A NUMBER FROM 1 TO 200"
20 P. "YOU GUESS WHAT IT IS IN TEN TURNS"
30 P. "OR LESS. HERE ARE THE QUESTIONS YOU MAY ASK:"
40 P. "1) IS X (COMPUTER NUMBER) GREATER THAN Y (A NUMBER
   YOU ENTER)?"
50 P. "2) IS X LESS THAN Y
60 P. "3) IS X EQUAL TO Y
65 P.:P.:X=RND(200):P. "I HAVE MY NUMBER"
70 IN. "PRESS ENTER TO CONTINUE ";A$:CLS
110 P. "THE CHOICES ARE:"
120 P. "1) X>Y
130 P. "2) X<Y
140 P. "3) X=Y"
145 T=T+1
147 P. "THIS IS GUESS #";T
150 IN. "ENTER THE NUMBER OF THE QUESTION YOU WISH TO
   ASK";A
200 ON A GOTO 500,600,700
500 IN. "IS X GREATER THAN WHAT NUMBER ";B
510 IF X>B G. 520
515 P. "------------ N O ------------"
517 G. 550
520 P. "------------ Y E S ------------"
550 IF T=10 G.800
560 G. 70
600 IN. "IS X LESS THAN WHAT NUMBER ";B
610 IF X<B G. 520
620 G. 515
700 IN. "IS X EQUAL TO WHAT NUMBER ";B
710 IF X=B G. 900
720 G. 515
800 P. "YOU ARE OUT OF GUESSES. MY NUMBER WAS ";X
810 END
900 P. "YES!--YOU HAVE WON WITH ";10-T;" GUESSES LEFT!"
910 END
```

Achille's Heel

Human and computer both have an army of 25 robots. In order to win, the player must find and destroy the computer's unknown control robot before the computer does likewise to his.

Variable List

B - Computer's control robot.

A - Human's control robot.

A(D) - Status of each of human's robots-been fired at yet or not.

Suggested Variations

■ Change number of control robots.
■ Change number of total robots.

Sample Run

THE ENEMY HAS SELECTED ITS CONTROL ROBOT.
WHICH ROBOT DO YOU DESIGNATE AS YOURS (1-25)?15
WHICH ROBOT DO YOU WISH TO FIRE AT?2
ROBOT #2 IS NOT THE ENEMY'S CONTROL ROBOT.
ENEMY FIRES AT ROBOT #24
OBVIOUSLY NOT YOUR CONTROL ROBOT--(15)
WHICH ROBOT DO YOU WISH TO FIRE AT?6
ROBOT #6 IS NOT THE ENEMY'S CONTROL ROBOT
ENEMY FIRES AT ROBOT #4
OBVIOUSLY NOT YOUR CONTROL ROBOT--(15)
WHICH ROBOT DO YOU WISH TO FIRE AT?11
HOORAY! YOU'VE KILLED THE ENEMY'S ARMY!

Program Listing

```
  5 CLS:P.:P.:P."ACHILLE'S HEEL":P.
  7 FOR D=1 TO 25:A(D)=1:N.D
 10 P. "THERE ARE TWO ARMIES OF ROBOTS- ONE CONTROLLED BY"
 20 P. "YOU, THE OTHER CONTROLLED BY THE ENEMY."
 30 P. "IN EACH ARMY THERE IS ONE CONTROL ROBOT WHICH"
 40 P. "ALL OTHER ROBOTS DEPEND UPON FOR SURVIVAL. DESTROY"
 50 P. "THIS ROBOT, AND YOU HAVE DESTROYED THE ENEMY."
 80 B=RND(25)
 90 P. "THE ENEMY HAS SELECTED IT'S CONTROL ROBOT."
100 IN. "WHICH ROBOT DO YOU DESIGNATE AS YOURS (1-25)";A
115 IF (A>=1)*(A<=25) G. 130
120 P. "ROBOTS ARE DESIGNATED BY THE NUMBERS 1 THROUGH 25"
125 G. 100
130 CLS:IN. "WHICH ROBOT DO YOU WISH TO FIRE AT";C
135 IF C=B G. 200
137 P. "ROBOT #";C;" IS NOT THE ENEMY'S CONTROL ROBOT"
140 D=RND(25):IF A(D)=0 G. 140
150 P. "ENEMY FIRES AT ROBOT #";D
153 IF D=A G. 210
154 A(D)=0
155 P. "OBVIOUSLY NOT YOUR CONTROL ROBOT--(";A;")"
160 IN. "PRESS ENTER TO CONTINUE ";A$:CLS: G. 130
200 P. "HOORAY!! YOU'VE KILLED THE ENEMY'S ARMY!"
205 END
210 P. "OH NO! HE'S KILLED YOUR CONTROL ROBOT AND DESTROYED"
215 P. "YOUR ARMY."
220 END
```

The Camel's Back

Two players choose unknown weights to place on the camel's back. When the weight on the camel's back exceeds 150 pounds, the player who placed the last weight on the camel's back loses.

Variable List

A$, B$ - Players' names.
A, B, C, D, E - Values of weights 1-5 respectively.
K - Used to see which player starts the game (as player 1).
W - How much weight on camel's back.
F - Player's weight choice.

Suggested Variations

■ Change breaking point as controlled in Line #160.
■ Change program to accomodate more than 2 players.
■ Change range of weights as controlled in Line #130.
■ Note system from Line #70 to 105. Can you apply the same "who goes first" principle to other multi-player programs?

Sample Run

ENTER ONE OF THE PLAYER'S FIRST NAME ? SCOTT
ENTER THE OTHER PLAYER'S FIRST NAME ? WATSON
WATSON IS PLAYER #1
SCOTT IS PLAYER #2
PRESS ENTER TO CONTINUE?
IT IS PLAYER #1'S TURN
THE CAMEL HAS 0 POUNDS ON HIS BACK
ENTER THE NUMBER OF THE WEIGHT YOU CHOOSE (1-5)?4
WEIGHT 4-- 4 LBS.

YOUR WEIGHTS LOOKED LIKE THIS:
WEIGHT 1 --- 12 LBS.
WEIGHT 2 --- 24 LBS.
WEIGHT 3 --- 12 LBS.
WEIGHT 4 --- 4 LBS.
WEIGHT 5 --- 1 LBS.
PRESS ENTER TO CONTINUE?
IT IS PLAYER #2'S TURN
THE CAMEL HAS 4 POUNDS ON HIS BACK
ENTER THE NUMBER OF THE WEIGHT YOU CHOOSE (1-5)?

Program Listing

```
  5 CLS:P.:P.:P."THE CAMEL'S BACK":P.
 10 W=0:G=1
 20 P. "YOU HAVE YOUR CHOICE OF 5 UNKNOWN WEIGHTS,"
 30 P. "NUMBERED 1-5, TO PLACE ON THE CAMEL'S BACK."
 40 P. "THE OBJECT IS TO FORCE YOUR OPPONENT TO"
 50 P. "BREAK THE CAMEL'S BACK BY EXCEEDING 150 LBS."
 60 P. "TOTAL WEIGHT."
 70 IN. "ENTER ONE OF THE PLAYER'S FIRST NAME ";A$
 80 IN. "ENTER THE OTHER PLAYER'S FIRST NAME ";B$
 90 K=RND(2):IF K=1 G. 100
 92 P. A$;" IS PLAYER #1"
 94 P. B$;" IS PLAYER #2"
 97 G. 110
100 P. B$;" IS PLAYER #1"
105 P. A$;" IS PLAYER #2"
110 IN. "PRESS ENTER TO CONTINUE ";A$:CLS
115 P. "IT IS PLAYER #";G;" 'S TURN"
120 P. "THE CAMEL HAS ";W;" LBS. ON ITS BACK."
130 A=RND(25):B=RND(25):C=RND(25):D=RND(25):E=RND(25)
140 IN. "ENTER THE NUMBER OF THE WEIGHT YOU CHOOSE (1-5)";F
145 IF (F<1)+(F>5) THEN P. "WEIGHTS ARE NUMBERED 1-5":G. 140
148 F=INT(F)
150 IF F=1 THEN W=W+A:P. "WEIGHT 1--";A;" LBS."
152 IF F=2 THEN W=W+B: P. "WEIGHT 2--";B;" LBS."
154 IF F=3 THEN W=W+C: P. "WEIGHT 3--";C;" LBS."
156 IF F=4 THEN W=W+D: P. "WEIGHT 4--";D;" LBS."
158 IF F=5 THEN W=W+E: P. "WEIGHT 5--";E;" LBS."
159 GOS. 1000
160 IF W>150 G. 200
170 IF G=1 THEN G=2:G. 110
180 IF G=2 THEN G=1:G. 110
200 P. "PLAYER #";G;"HAS BROKEN THE CAMEL'S BACK"
210 P. "WITH ";W;" LBS. TOTAL."
220 IF G=1 THEN X=2
230 IF G=2 THEN X=1
240 P. "PLAYER #";X;" IS THE WINNER!"
250 END
1000 P. "YOUR WEIGHTS LOOKED LIKE THIS:"
1010 P. "WEIGHT 1 --- ";A;" LBS."
1020 P. "WEIGHT 2 --- ";B;" LBS."
1030 P. "WEIGHT 3 --- ";C;" LBS."
1040 P. "WEIGHT 4 --- ";D;" LBS."
1050 P. "WEIGHT 5 --- ";E;" LBS."
1060 RETURN
```

84

Kamikaze

Player must use his remaining ammo wisely in order to destroy five enemy kamikaze planes. The weapon will continue to fire until either the plane is destroyed or the ammo is depleted.

Variable List

N - Kamikaze number.
M - Rounds of machine gun ammo.
S - Number of ship to air shells.
K - Player's choice of weapons.
Z- Whether machine gun ammo hits or not.
K - Whether shells hit or not.
X - Time delay loop.

Suggested Variations

■ Change amount of starting ammo as controlled in Line #90.
■ Change number of kamikazes by increasing or decreasing the FOR-NEXT loop in Line #100.
■ Change effectiveness of each weapon as controlled in Line #'s 150 and 230.

Sample Run

```
KAMIKAZE # 1 IS DIVING!
ENTER 1 FOR GUNS OR 2 FOR SHELLS ?2
SSHHH....
          SPLUT
SSHHH....
KA-BLOOEY!!--KAMIKAZE #1 DESTROYED!
AMMO REPORT
200 ROUNDS MACHINE GUN AMMO
8 SHIP TO AIR SHELLS
PRESS ENTER TO CONTINUE?
KAMIKAZE # 2 IS DIVING!
ENTER 1 FOR GUNS OR 2 FOR SHELLS ?1
BLAT-A
BLAT-A
BLAT-A
BLAT-A
BLAT-A
KA-POW!--KAMIKAZE #2 DESTROYED!
AMMO REPORT
195 ROUNDS MACHINE GUN AMMO
8 SHIP TO AIR SHELLS
PRESS ENTER TO CONTINUE?
```

Program Listing

```
  5 CLS:P.:P.:P."KAMIKAZE":P.
 10 P. "AFTER A HEAVY BATTLE AT SEA, YOUR AMMO"
 20 P. "IS SEVERELY LOW. ON YOUR WAY BACK"
 30 P. "TO PORT, 5 KAMIKAZE PLANES ARE SIGHTED."
 40 P. "YOU HAVE YOUR CHOICE OF TWO WEAPONS TO USE, BUT"
 50 P. "MUST CONTINUE FIRING THEM UNTIL YOU HIT THE PLANE."
 60 P. "YOUR AMMO STANDS AS FOLLOWS:"
 70 P. "200 ROUNDS MACHINE GUN AMMO"
 80 P. "10 SHIP TO AIR SHELLS"
 90 P.:M=200:S=10
100 FOR N=1 TO 5
105 IN. "PRESS ENTER TO CONTINUE ";A$:CLS
110 P. "KAMIKAZE #";N;" IS DIVING!"
120 IN. "ENTER 1 FOR GUNS OR 2 FOR SHELLS";K
140 IF K=2 G. 200
142 IF M=0 G. 145
143 G. 150
145 P. "GUNS OUT OF AMMO. GOING TO SHELLS."
147 G. 200
150 Z=RND(50):IF Z=25 G. 170
152 CLS:FOR X=1 TO 50:N. X
155 P. "BLAT-A"
157 M=M-1
160 IF M=0 G. 2000
165 G. 150
170 P. "KA-POW!--KAMIKAZE #";N;" DESTROYED!"
172 M=M-1
175 G. 1000
200 IF S=0 G. 210
205 G. 220
210 P. "SHELLS DEPLETED, GOING TO GUNS"
215 IF (M=0)*(S=0) G. 2000
217 G. 150
220 P. "SSHHH..."
225 FOR X=1 TO 500:N. X
230 K=RND(4):IF K=2 G. 270
231 P. "        SPLUT"
233 FOR X=1 TO 250:N. X
235 S=S-1
237 IF S=0 G. 2000
240 G. 220
270 P. "KA-BLOOEY!--KAMIKAZE #";N;" DESTROYED!"
280 S=S-1
1000 P. "AMMO REPORT"
1010 P. M; " ROUNDS MACHINE GUN AMMO"
1020 P. S;" SHIP TO AIR SHELLS"
1030 N. N
1040 P. "YOU'VE DESTROYED THEM ALL! YOU WIN!"
1070 END
2000 P. "OH NO! YOU'VE RUN OUT OF AMMO DURING BATTLE"
2010 P "AND HAVE BEEN BLOWN TO SMITHEREENS!"
2020 END
```

Chapter 6
Graphics Programs

One of the aesthetically pleasing features of the microcomputer is its ability to format and produce an eye catching display. The programs in this section are dedicated to producing, or at least simulating, some of the finest graphics programs available. As you will see, some of the programs come quite close to the popular video games that gobble quarters by the dozens daily.

For modification purposes, or for conversion to other forms of BASIC, it is important to define and explain the video format used in these programs. The video screen is divided up into many small rectangles that are accessable by a graphics location. The X axis (horizontal) is divided into 128 units numbered 0 to 127. The Y axis (vertical) is divided into 48 units numbered 0 to 47. From these divisions, we can see that there are 6144 "blocks" that can be used to draw pictures, lines, or whatever. The command SET (X, Y) will darken the block at coordinates X, Y. The command RESET (X, Y) will light the block at coordinates X, Y. In order to find out whether a particular graphic location is lit or not, we use the command POINT(X, Y). This command will return a 1 if the block at coordinates X, Y is lit or a 0 if it is not.

In order to print alpha-numeric data at a particular location on the screen, we use the command PRINT AT X or P.ATX. Print locations on the video screen are numbered 0 (upper left-hand corner of the screen) to 1023 (lower right-hand corner of the screen). If we wished to print the character * on the last position of the first line from the top of the screen (Print location #63) we would use the statement 10 PRINT AT 63, "*".

It would be to your advantage to either make or buy some video worksheets if you plan to do any modifications or conversions of these programs.

Electric Crayon

Using a direction system, the user can draw figures, graphs, or lines. Remember that the top line of the screen is used for the input statement "WHAT DIRECTION (1 TO 8)" when you choose your starting X and Y coordinates. See Fig. 6-1.

Variable List

X, Y - Leading point.
D - Entered desired direction.

Suggested Variations

■ Add a command to delete graphics blocks in a desired direction.

■ Since drawing a figure block by block can be slow and tedious, you may wish to add a command to print more than one block at a time. For example, entering 2,10 would print 10 squares in the direction 2.

Program Listing

```
  5 CLS:P.:P.:P."ELECTRIC CRAYON":P.
 40 P. "THIS PROGRAM WILL ENABLE YOU TO USE THE COMPUTER'S"
 50 P. "GRAPHIC FUNCTIONS TO DRAW FIGURES, GRAPHS,
    OR WHATEVER."
 60 P.
 70 P. "IN ORDER TO CONTINUE THE LINE, JUST ENTER THE"
 80 P. "APPROPRIATE DIRECTION INDEX AS SHOWN ON THE MAP
    BELOW:"
 90 P.
100 P. "      8  1  2"
110 P. "      7  ×  3"
120 P. "      6  5  4"
130 P.
140 P. "WHERE THE LETTER X REPRESENTS YOUR LEADING POINT."
150 IN. "PRESS ENTER TO BEGIN ";A$:CLS
160 IN. "ENTER YOUR STARTING X COORDINATE (0 TO 127) ";X
170 IN. "ENTER YOUR STARTING Y COORDINATE (0 TO 47) ";Y
180 IF (X< 0)+(X> 127) G. 160
190 IF (Y< 0)+(Y> 47) G. 170
200 SET(X,Y)
210 P.ATO,"WHAT DIRECTION (1 TO 8) ";:IN. D
220 IF (D<1)+(D>8) G. 210
221 ON D G. 300,400,500,600,700,800,900,1000
222 REM *** PLOT DESIRED POINT
300 REM *** 1 COMMAND
301 Y=Y-1:SET(X,Y)
302 G. 210
400 REM *** 2 COMMAND
401 X=X+1:Y=Y-1
405 SET(X,Y)
410 G. 210
500 REM *** 3 COMMAND
501 X=X+1:SET(X,Y)
505 G. 210
600 REM *** 4 COMMAND
601 X=X+1:Y=Y+1
605 SET(X,Y)
610 G. 210
700 REM *** 5 COMMAND
```

ENTER YOUR STARING X COORDINATE (0 TO 127)?63
ENTER YOUR STARTING Y COORDINATE (0 TO 47)?23_

WHAT DIRECTION (1 TO 8)?2_

WHAT DIRECTION (1 TO 8)?3_

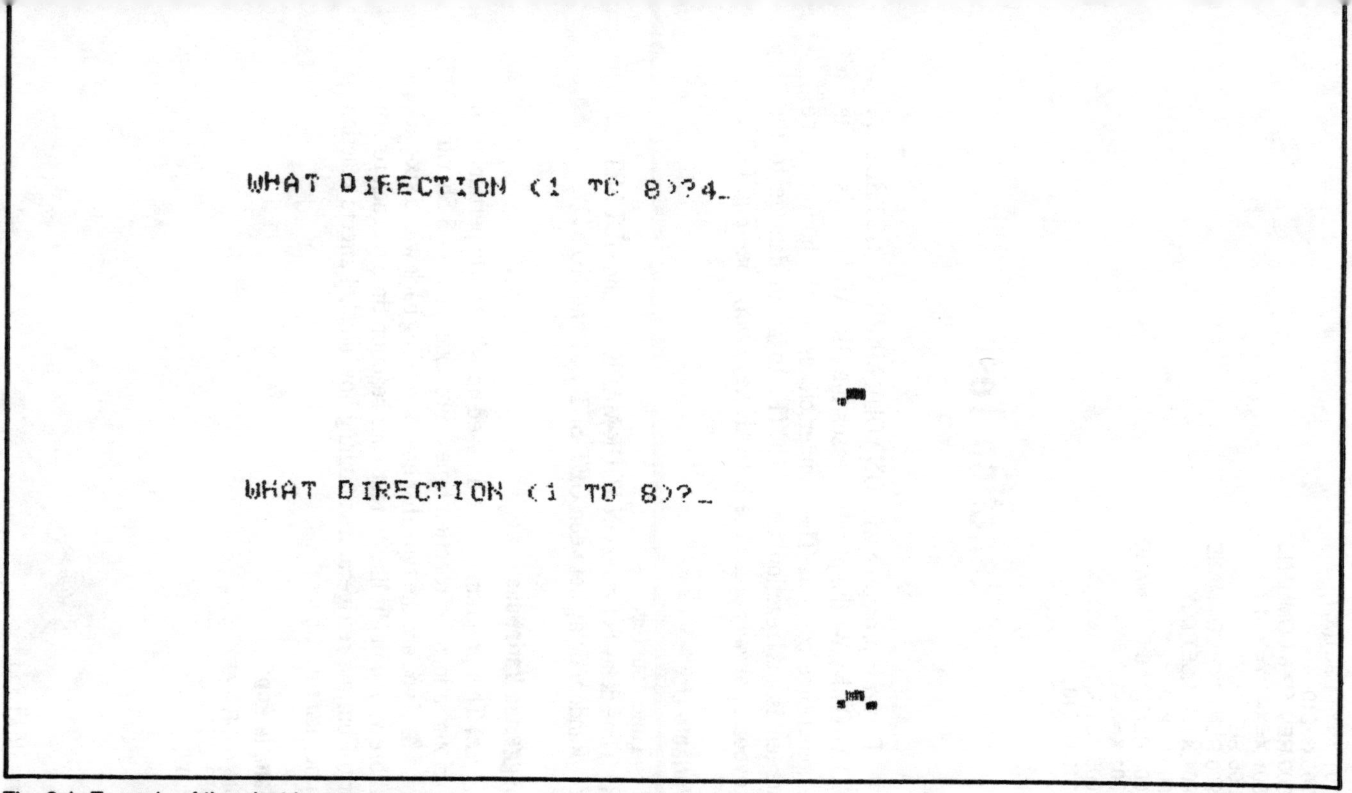

WHAT DIRECTION (1 TO 8)?4_

WHAT DIRECTION (1 TO 8)??_

Fig. 6-1. Example of the electric crayon.

```
701 Y=Y+1:SET(X,Y)
705 G. 210
800 REM *** 6 COMMAND
801 X=X-1:Y=Y+1
805 SET (X,Y)
900 REM *** 7 COMMAND
901 X=X-1:SET (X,Y)
905 G. 210
1000 REM *** 8 COMMAND
1001 X=X-1: Y=Y-1
1005 SET(X,Y)
1010 G. 210
```

Reaction Test

Player is prompted with ON YOUR MARK . . . GET SET . . . NOW! On NOW! the player presses the BREAK key to stop the elapsed time counter. The number closest to the bottom of the screen is his reaction time. NOTE: to avoid damage to the keyboard, always press the BREAK key *gently*. See Fig. 6-2.

Variable List

T - Time counter.
R - Time delay between ON YOUR MARK . . . and GET SET . . .
Y - Random delay between GET SET . . . and NOW!

Suggested Variations

■ This program can be dressed up with charts pertaining to various ratings for reaction times. For example: 0 - 3 Sheriff.

■ If you are the type that enjoys settling back with a six-pack of brew, you might like to test your reaction time on each return trip from the refrigerator. Stunning how alcohol affects reaction time, isn't it? Cheers!

Sample Run

```
ON YOUR MARK . . .
GET SET . . .
NOW!
1
2
3
4
5
6
BREAK AT 120
```

92

Program Listing

```
  1 CLS:P.:P.:P."REACTION TIMER":P.
  5 T=0
 10 P. "KEEP YOUR HAND ON THE BREAK KEY!"
 20 P. "WHEN THE WORD NOW! APPEARS, PRESS THE BREAK KEY
       GENTLY"
 30 P. "TO STOP THE TIMER. THE LAST NUMBER (CLOSEST TO THE"
 40 P. "BOTTOM OF THE SCREEN) IS YOUR REACTION TIME."
 50 P.:IN. "PRESS ENTER TO START THE COUNTDOWN;A$:CLS
 60 P "ON YOUR MARK . . ."
 70 FOR R=1TO1000:N. R
 75 CLS:P. "GET SET . . . . . "
 80 Y=RND(2500)
 85 FOR V=1 TO Y:N. V
 90 CLS:P. "NOW!"
100 T=T+1
110 P. T
120 G. 100
```

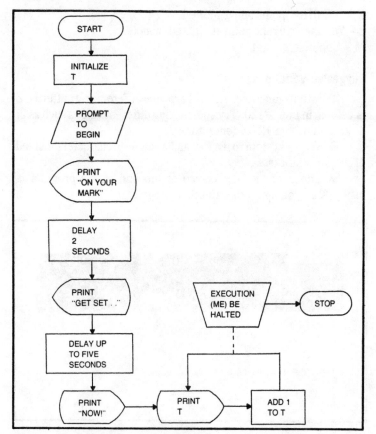

Fig. 6-2. Flowchart for the Reaction Timer.

The Random Rug

Well, it's either an old Indian-type rug or a punched FOR-TRAN card. If you look closely, you can see little shapes and figures in the rug. Kinda like staring at clouds. See Fig. 6-3.

Variable List

X,Y - Current point being plotted.
Z - Whether current point is lighted or not.
M - Continue or quit.

Suggested Variations

■ Various functions of Z will produce different rug patterns. Z is defined in Line #120. Try substituting different values such as 2, 3, and 5 into the RND generator.

■ Write a system to display alpha-numeric characters instead of graphics blocks.

■ The continue/quit choice at the end of the program is handy. Can you apply this to other programs?

INPUT 1 FOR NEW RUG OR 2 TO QUIT?2

Fig. 6-3. Example of the Random Rug.

Program Listing

```
  5 CLS:P.:P.:P."THE RANDOM RUG":P.
 10 P. "THROUGH THE MIRACLES OF MODERN TECHNOLOGY, THIS
    PROGRAM"
 20 P. "WILL GENERATE A 'RUG' PATTERN BEFORE YOUR VERY EYES!"
 50 IN. "PRESS ENTER TO BEGIN ";A$:CLS
100 FOR Y=1 TO 44
110 FOR X=1 TO 127
120 Z=RND(4)
130 IF Z=2 G. 150
140 SET (X,Y)
150 N. X
160 N. Y
170 P.AT960,"ENTER 1 FOR NEW RUG OR 2 TO QUIT";:IN. M
175 IF M=2 G. 185
180 CLS:G. 100
185 END
```

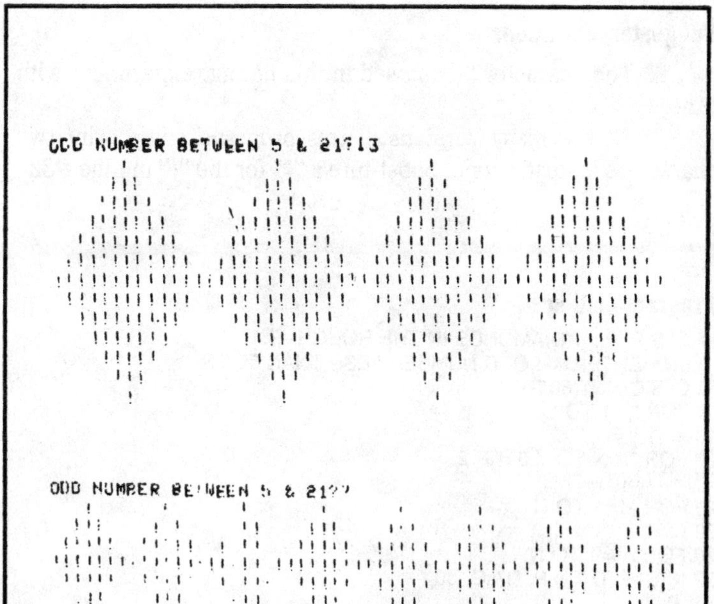

Fig. 6-4. Example of Diamonds in the Rough.

Diamonds In The Rough

Now we're getting fancy, eh? The entered odd number controls how many diamonds are printed horizontally, the vertical length of each diamond, and the number of diamonds printed vertically. See Fig. 6-4.

Variable List

R - Odd number entered.
N - Printing loop.
X, Y, Z - Parameters of printing loop.
M, A - Used in calculating printing position.

Suggested Variations

■ The character "!" is used in this listing, experiment with others.

■ Of the many versions of this program, some print two characters instead of one. Substitute a "*" for the "!" in Line #32

Program Listing

```
1 CLS:P.:P.:P."DIAMONDS IN THE ROUGH":P.
5. IN. "ENTER AN ODD NUMBER LESS THAN 50 ";R
6 CLS:Q=INT(60/R)
8 FOR L=1 TO Q
10 X=1:Y=R:Z=2
20 FOR N=X TO Y STEP 2
25 P.TAB((R−N)/2);
28 FOR M=1 TO Q
29 C=1
30 FOR A =1 TO N
32 IF C>2 THEN P. "!";:G. 50
34. P. "!"
36 C=C+1
50 N.A
53 IF M=Q G. 60
55 P.TAB(R*M*+(R−N)/2);
56 N. M
60 P.
70 N. N
83 IF X<> 1 G. 95
85 X=R−2:Y=1:Z=−2
90 G.20
95 N. L
99 END
```

Zig Zag

I don't know why, but this is a great attention grabbing program, as well as an effective pacifier.

Variable List

A$-First string.
B$-Second string.
I-Tab increment.
L-Left margin boundary.
R-Right margain boundary.
Z-Time delay loop.

Suggested Variations

■ Here's a toughy—add a system to print 2 zig zags each opposing the other to produce a printout like:

```
     X
   X   X
     X X
       X
   X X
 X   X
```

Sample Run

INPUT THE FIRST STRING, UP TO 16 CHARACTERS?HELLO
INPUT THE SECOND STRING?THERE
WHAT IS THE INCREMENT?10
WHAT IS THE LEFT MARGIN BOUNDARY (0 TO 23)?5
WHAT IS THE RIGHT MARGIN BOUNDARY (24 TO 47)?47
WHAT IS THE TIME INTERVAL (SMALL NUMBER FOR FAST DISPLAY)?50
```
    HELLO
        HELLO
            HELLO
                HELLO
                    HELLO
                        THERE
                    THERE
                THERE
            THERE
        THERE
HELLO
    HELLO
        HELLO
```

Program Listing

```
85 CLS:P.:P.:P."ZAG ZAG":P.
20 IN. "INPUT THE FIRST STRING, UP TO 16 CHARACTERS ";A$
```

```
30 IN. "INPUT THE SECOND STRING ";B$
40 IN. "WHAT IS THE INCREMENT ";I
50 IN. "WHAT IS THE LEFT MARGIN BOUNDARY (0 TO 23) ";L
60 IN. "WHAT IS THE RIGHT MARGIN BOUNDARY (24 TO 47)";R
65 IN. "WHAT IS THE TIME INTERVAL (SMALL NUMBER FOR FAST
    DISPLAY)";Z
70 CLS:P. "WAIT TILL YOU SEE THIS!":FOR T= 1 TO 1000:N T:CLS
80 Q=L
100 P.TAB(Q);A$
105 FOR Y=1 TO Z:N. Y
110 Q=Q+I
120 OF Q>=R G. 200
130 G. 100
200 P.TAB(Q);B$
205 FOR Y=1 TO Z:N. Y
210 Q=Q-I
220 IF Q<=L G. 100
230 B. 200
```

Sine Wave Manipulation

This program prints a sine wave on your display according to
your specified frequency and amplitude. Not only is this a good
program to sit back and watch, it is also an excellant teaching tool.
See Fig. 6-5.

Variable List

B$ - Plotting character.
B - Frequency.
G - Amplitude.
A - Printing loop.
C - Printing tabulator.
Z, X, Y - Used in sine subroutine.

Suggested Variations

■ An "*" is used for plotting in this listing. Try other characters, or even an entered string.

■ Think about this one awhile—devise a system which alter-
nates printing two entered strings.
■ Try other subroutines like cosine or tangent.

Sample Run

ENTER THE DESIRED FREQUENCY ?25
ENTER THE DESIRED AMPLITUDE ?25

98

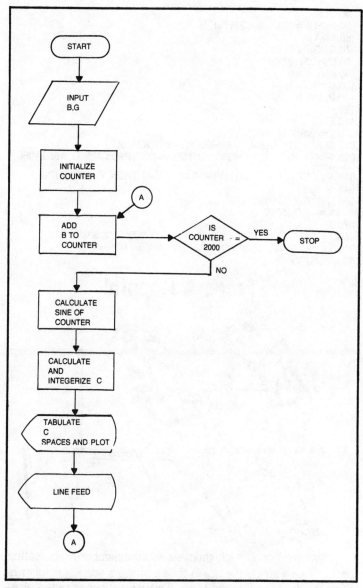

Fig. 6-5. Flowchart for the Sine Wave Manipulation.

Program Listing

```
 5 CLS:P.:P.:P."SINE WAVE MANIPULATION":P.
10 B$=*
20 IN. "ENTER THE DESIRED FREQUENCY ";B
30 IN. "ENTER THE DESIRED AMPLITUDE ";G
```

```
   40 CLS
   50 FOR A=0 TO 20000 STEP B
   60 X=A
   70 GOS. 1000
   80 C=(32+(G*Y))
   90 C=C+.5
  100 C=INT(C)
  110 P.TAB (C);B$
  120 N. A
  130 END
 1000 Z=ABS(X)/X:X=Z*X
 1010 IF X > 360 THEN X=X/360:X=(X-INT(X))*360
 1020 IF X > 90 Then X=X/90:Y=INT(X):X=(X-Y)*90:ON Y G. 1050,1060,
      1070
 1030 X=X/57.29578: IF ABS(X) < 2.48616E-4 THEN Y=0:RETURN
 1040 G. 1080
 1050 X=90-X:G. 1030
 1060 X=-X:G. 1030
 1070 X=X-90:G. 1030
 1080 Y=X-X*X*X/6+X*X*X*X*X/120-X*X*X*X*X*X*X/5040
 1090 Y=Y+X*X*X*X*X*X*X*X*X/362880: IF Z=-1 THEN Y=-Y
 1100 RETURN
```

Frogs A Hoppin'

Players (1 or 2) each choose a scoring number representing the spots on a single die. Each time a player's scoring number is rolled, his frog is advanced 1 hop. Thirty five hops wins the race. Five races are run in a match.

Variable List

N - Number of players.

A - Player's 1's scoring number.

B - Player 2's scoring number.

S - Player 1's frog's position.

T - Player 2's frog's position.

U - Player 1's die.

V - Player 2's die.

X - Round number.

J - Number of games won by player 1.

K - Number of games won by player 2.

Suggested Variations

■ Change number of races in a match as controlled in line #95.

■ Allow more than 2 participants.

```
Race # 1
SCOTT, WHAT IS YOUR SCORING NUMBER ?4
MY SCORING NUMBER IS 6
TYPE IN A NUMBER TO BEGIN THE RACE?20
-------------------------------------------------------------------------------
SCOTT          ****                                                      F
                                                                         I
                                                                         N
                                                                         I
                                                                         S
COMPUTER       ##                                                        H
SCOTT'S DIE- 1                                     COMPUTER'S DIE- 4
-------------------------------------------------------------------------------
SCOTT          **************************** *****************************  F
                                                                         I
                                                                         N
                                                                         I
                                                                         S
COMPUTER       ####################################
SCOTT'S DIE- 6                                     COMPUTER'S DIE- 6
COMPUTER'S FROG WINS! TYPE A NUMBER TO CONTINUE?
```

Program Listing

```
5 CLS:P.:P.:P."FROGS A HOPPIN'":P.
10 P. "IN THIS GAME, EACH PARTICIPANT CHOOSES A SCORING"
20 P. "NUMBER FROM 1 TO 6, REPRESENTING THE SPOTS ON A"
30 P. "SINGLE DIE. EACH TIME HIS NUMBER IS ROLLED, HIS"
40 P. "FROG WILL BE ADVANCED 1 HOP. THIRTY FIVE HOPS WIND
   THE"
50 P. "RACE. FIVE RACES ARE RUN IN A MATCH.":P.
55 J=0 K=0
60 P.:IN. "HOW MANY PLAYERS (1 OR 2)";N
70 IF (N > 2)+(N < 1) THEN P. "INPUT ERROR":G. 60
80.IN. "WHAT IS PLAYER 1'S NAME ";A$
85 IF N=1 THEN B$="COMPUTER":G. 95
90 IN. "WHAT IS PLAYER 2'S NAME ";B$
95 FOR X=1 TO 5:CLS:P. "RACE #";X:P.:P.
```

```
100 P. A$;", WHAT IS YOUR SCORING NUMBER ";:IN. A
110 IF N=1 THEN B=RND(6):P. "MY SCORING NUMBER IS ";B:G. 130
120 P. B$;", WHAT IS YOUR SCORING NUMBER ";:IN. B
130 IF (A>0)*(A<7)*(B>0)*(B<7) G. 140
135 P. "INPUT ERROR":G. 100
140 IN "TYPE A NUMBER TO BEGIN THE RACE ";Z
145 CLS
150 S=335:T=655
152 PAT320,A$;:P.AT640,B$;
154 P.AT369, "F";:P.AT433,"I";:P.AT497,"N";
156 P.AT561,"I";:P.AT625,"S";:P.AT689,"H";
160 P.ATS,"#";:P.ATT,"*";
180 U=RND(6):V=RND(6)
185 P.AT896,A$;'"S DIE—";U;:P.AT931,B$;'"S DIE—";V;
190 IF U=A THEN S=S+1
200 IF V=B THEN T=T+1
210 P.ATS,"#";:P.ATT,"*";
220 IF (S=369)*(T=369)6.250
230 G. 180
250 IF (S=369)*(T=689) G. 300
255 IF T=689 THEN P.:G. 280
257 P.
260 P.A$:'"S FROG WINS! TYPE A NUMBER TO CONTINUE";
265 IN. Z:J=J+1:N. X
270 CLS:P. "FINAL SCORE"
272 P. A$"------------ ";J
274 P.B$;"------------ ";K
276 END
280 P. B$'"S FROG WINS! TYPE A NUMBER TO CONTINUE";
290 IN. Z:K=K+1:N. X
295 G. 270
300 P. "I DON'T BELIEVE IT!! IT'S A DEAD TIE!"
310 P. "TYPE A NUMBER TO CONTINUE ";:IN.Z:N.X:G. 270
```

Putting Practice

Player tries to sink the ball in the cup by entering the right putter swing potency. To avoid wrap around, the ball is moved the same distance to the left of the hole in case of an overswing. See Fig. 6-6.

Variable List

M - Number of holes to be played.
L - Hole number.
X, Y, Z - Used to print the hole.
V, U - Used to print the ball.
Q - Stroke number for each hole.
P - Potency of shot.
G - Loop to print movement of ball for an underswing.
H - Loop to print movement of ball for an overswing.
N - Loop to print movement of ball for an exact swing.
O - Total strokes.

HOLE # 1

STROKE # 1
POTENCY (0 TO 127)>80_

HOLE # 1

STROKE # 2
POTENCY (0 TO 127)>10_

STROKE # 3
POTENCY (0 TO 127)?2_

HOLE # 1

STROKE # 3
POTENCY (0 TO 127)?8

HOLE # 1

IN THE CUP!

FINAL SCORE
HOLES PLAYED----- 1
PAR FOR 1 HOLES---- 3
YOUR TOTAL STROKES---- 3

READY
>_

Fig. 6-6. Example of Putting Practice.

Suggested Variation

■ Extend the starting distance range from the ball to the hole.

■ Vary the par for each hole according to starting distance.

Program Listing

```
  5 CLS:P.:P.:P."PUTTING PRACTICE":P.
 10 P."THE PLAYER MUST HIT THE HOLE (INDENTIFIED BY";
 15 P."THE H)"
 20. P. "BY ENTERING A PUTTER SWING POTENCY FROM 0 TO 127
     THAT WOULD"
 30 P. "PLACE THE BALL EXACTLY IN THE HOLE. AN OVERSWING
     THAT"
 35 0=0
 40 P. "WOULD PUTT THE BALL PAST THE HOLE WILL BE MOVED THE"
 50 P. "SAME DISTANCE TO THE NEAR(LEFT HAND)SIDE OF THE HOLE"
 55. P.:IN. "HOW MANY HOLES DO YOU WISH TO PLAY ";M
 57 FOR L=1 TO M
 60. P.AT896,"PRESS ENTER TO CONTINUE";:IN.A$:CLS
 65 Q=0
 70 Y=22: X=RND(50)+70
 75 T=1
 80 SET (X,Y)
 90 Z=448+X/2+2):P.ATZ,"H"
100 U=22:V=RND(25)
110 SET (V,U)
130 Q=Q+1:P.AT0,"STROKE #":Q
131 P.AT30,"HOLE#";L
132 P.AT64,"POTENCE (0 TO 127)";:IN.P
133 IF V+P<X G. 140
134 IF V+P>X G. 200
136 IF V+P=X G. 300
140 FOR G=1 TO P
145 V=V+1:SET(V,U):RESET(V-1,U)
160 N. G
170 G. 130
200 T=0
205 FOR H=1 TO P
207 IF T=1 G. 230
210 V=V+1:IF POINT (V+1,U)=1 G. 230
220 SET (V,U):RESET(V-1,U)
225 G. 250
230 T=1:V=V-1:SET(V,U):RESET(V+1,U)
250 N. H
260 G. 130
300 FOR N=1 TO P
310 V=V+1:SET(V,U):RESET(V-1,U)
320 N. N
330 P.AT412, "IN THE CUP!"
340 0=0+Q
360 N. L
1000 FOR X=1 TO 1000:N. X:CLS
1100 P. "FINAL SCORE"
1200 P. "HOLES PLAYED----- ";L-1
1250 P. "PAR FOR ";L-1;" HOLES---- ";(L-1)*3
1260 P. "YOUR TOTAL STROKES----- ";0
1270 END
```

Cannon

Player tries to hit a horizontal target by entering the right potency for the shot. This can be a tough game! See Fig. 6-7.

Variable List

K - Number of rounds to be played.

B - Round number.

H, I - Used in drawing target.

U, V, T, W - Used in drawing the cannon. U, V is later used to plot the movement of the cannonball.

Q - Loop to print movement of cannonball.

G - Number of hits scored by player.

Suggested Variations

■ Make the target larger.

■ Move the cannon each turn either horizontally or vertically.

■ Simulate a graphic explosion when a target is hit.

Program Listing

```
  5 CLS:P.:P.:P."CANNON":P.
 10 P. "IN THIS GAME, YOU MUST TRY TO HIT THE HORIZONTAL"
 20 P. "TARGET WITH A CANNONBALL BY ENTERING JUST THE RIGHT"
 30 P. "POTENCY FOR THE SHOT."
 35 G=0
 40 IN. "HOW MANY ROUNDS DO YOU WISH TO PLAY ";K
 60 FOR B=1 TO K
 70 IN. "PRESS ENTER TO CONTINUE ";A$:CLS
 80 P.AT35,"ROUND #";B
100 H=RND(124):IF H<50 G. 100
110 I=31
120 SET(H,I):SET(H+1,I):SET(H+2,I):SET(H+3,I)
130 FOR U=0 TO 7
140 V=20:SET(U,V)
150 N. U
160 FOR T=0 TO 3
170 W=21:SET(T,W)
180 N. T
190 P.AT704," "
200 P.AT0,"POTENCY (43 TO 120)";:IN. P
205 A=0
210 FOR Q=1 TO P
215 IF Q>=P-22 G. 300
220 U=U+1:SET(U,V):RESET(U-1,V)
230 N.Q
300 IF A=1 G. 350
310 A=1:RESET(U,V)
320 U=U+2:V=V+1:SET(U,V)
```

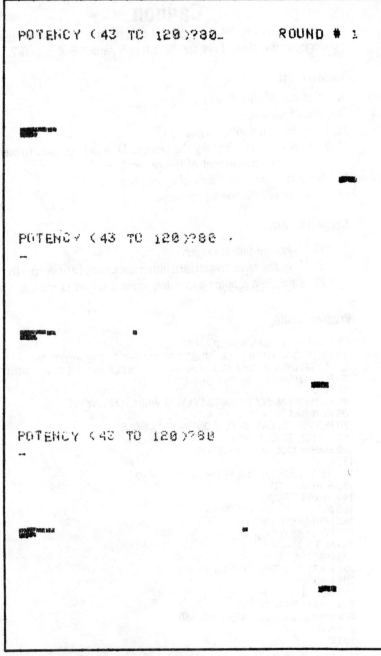

POTENCY (43 TO 120)?80_   ROUND # 1

POTENCY (43 TO 120)?80 .

POTENCY (43 TO 120)?80

Fig. 6-7. Example of the Cannon program.

POTENCY (43 TO 120)?80

POTENCY (43 TO 120)?80

POTENCY (43 TO 120)?80

SPLUT
GAME OVER. PRESS ENTER FOR SCOREBOARD?_

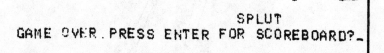

```
330 G. 230
350 U=U+2:V=V+1:SET(U,V):RESET(U-2,V-1)
360 IF V+1=31 G. 380
370 G. 230
380 IF POINT (U+2,V+1)=1 G. 390
381 IF POINT (U+1,V+1)=1 G. 390
382 U=U+2:V=V+1:SET(U,V):RESET(U-2,V-1):P.AT729,"SPLUT"
385 G. 490
390 RESET(U,V):P.AT729,"KA-BLAM! GOOD SHOT!"
400 G=G+1
490 N. B
500 IN. "GAME OVER. PRESS ENTER FOR SCOREBOARD";A$:CLS
510 P. "OUT OF ";B-1;" TARGETS YOU HIT ";G
520 P."FOR A TOTAL OF";G/(B-1)*100;"%"
530 END
```

Basketballer

Player tries to put the basketball in the basket by entering the correct potency for the shot. See Fig. 6-8.

Variable List

E - Number of rounds to be played.

F - Round number

X, Y - Used in drawing player. S, Y later used to plot movement of the basketball.

U, V - Used in drawing basket.

A, B, C, D, - Used in drawing boundaries.

I - Number of baskets made by player.

Suggested Variations

■ Deduct points for using the backboard.

■ Extend the range of the man as controlled in Line #100.

■ Raise or lower the basket each turn.

Basketballer

```
5 CLS:P.:P.:P."BASKETBALLER":P.
7 I=0
10 P. "IN THIS GAME, YOU TRY TO PUT THE BALL IN THE BASKET"
20 P. "BY ENTERING THE CORRECT SHOT POTENCY."
30 "HOW MANY ROUNDS DO YOU WISH TO PLAY";E
40 FOR F=1 TO E
45 P.AT390,"PRESS ENTER TO CONTINUE";:IN. A$:CLS
90 P.AT1,-"ROUND #";F
100 Y=44:X=RND(120):IF X<47 G. 100
110 SET(X,Y):SET(X+1,Y:SET(X+3,Y)
120 SET(X+2,Y+1):SET(X+3,Y+1)
130 SET(X+3,Y+2)
150 FOR U=0 TO 8
160 V=39
170 SET(U,V)
180 N.U
190 SET(2,40):SET(7,40):SET(3,41):SET(6,41):SET(4,42):SET(5,42)
192 FOR A=6 TO 47:B=0:SET(B,A):N. A
195 FOR C=1 TO 127:D=47:SET(C,D):N. C
200 P.AT12,"POTENCY";:IN. P
205 R=0:G=0
210 IF R>=P/2+6 G. 300
215 R=R+1
216 IF X-3<0 THEN RESET(X,Y):X=1:SET(X,Y):G. 300
218 IF POINT(X-1,Y-1)=1 G. 355
220 X=X-3:Y=Y-1
230 SET(X,Y):RESET(X+3,Y+1)
240 G 210
300 IF G=1 G. 308
```

111

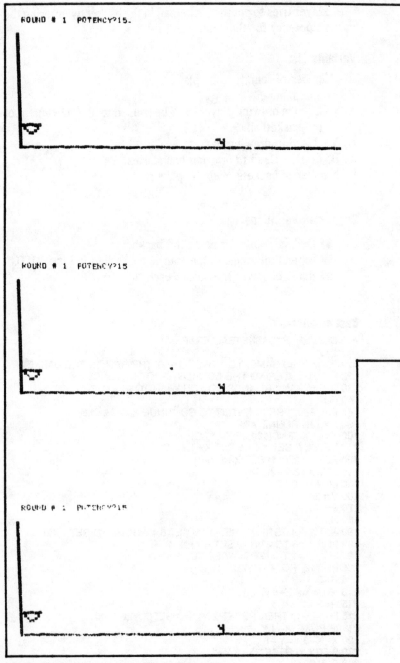

Fig. 6-8. Example of the Basektballer program.

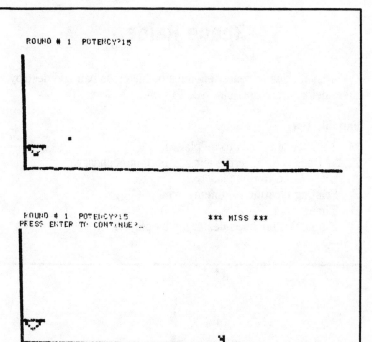

```
302 G=:RESET(X,Y)
308 X=X-3:Y=Y+1
309 IF X<=0 THEN X=X+1:G. 309
310 SET(X,Y)
320 RESET(X+3,Y-1):RESET(X+2,Y-1):RESET(X+1,Y-1)
330 IF POINT(X-1,Y+1)=1 G. 350
332 IF POINT(X-2,Y+1)=1G. 350
340 G. 210
350 IF Y=38 G. 400
352 IF Y>38 G. 390
355 RESET(X,Y)
357 X=X+1:Y=Y+1:SET(X,Y):RESET(X-1,Y-1)
360 IF POINT (X+1,Y+1)=1 G. 350
370 G. 357
390 P.AT38,"*** MISS ***"
395 G. 600
400 P.AT38,"*** 2 POINTS1 ***"
410 I=I+1
600 N. F
610 IN. "PRESS ENTER TO CONTINUE";A$:CLS
620 P. OUT OF ";F-1;" SHOTS, YOU MADE ";I
630 P. "FOR A TOTAL OF ";I/(F-1)*100;"% FROM THE FIELD"
640 END
```

113

Space Raider

Player tries to center enemies on his cross hair and destroy them before time runs out. See Fig. 6-9.

Variable List

M - Number of rounds to be played.
X, Y - Used to draw crosshair and bottom boundary.
A, B, C - Used to draw laser.
R - Printing position for enemy symbol (*).
H - Time.
O - Number of enemies destroyed by player.

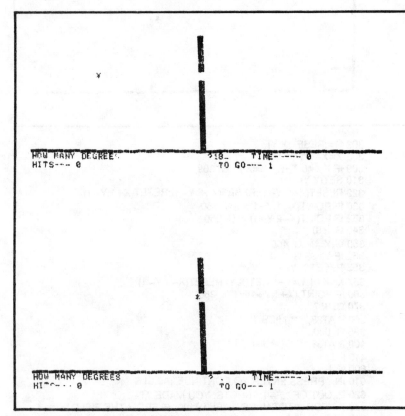

Fig. 6-9. Example of the Space Raider program.

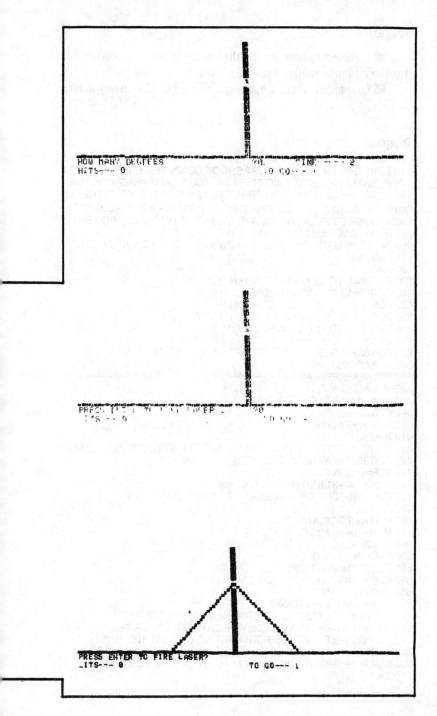

Suggested Variations

■ Devise a system so that the enemy is not only plotted and positioned horizontally, but also vertically.

■ Graphically simulate an explosion when the enemy is hit.

Program Listing

```
  5 CLS:P.:P.:P."SPACE RAIDER":P.
 10 P."IN THIS GAME, YOU MUST SHOOT DOWN THE ENEMY SPACE"
 20 P."SHIPS BY CENTERING THEM ON YOUR CROSSHAIR.POSITIVE"
 30 P. "DEGREES MOVE THE TARGET TO THE RIGHT OF YOUR SCREEN,"
 40 P. "NEGATIVE DEGREES TO THE LEFT. ENTER 0 DEGREES TO"
 50 P. "ARM YOUR LASER. AN AVERAGE OF 3 TIME UNITS PER ENEMY"
 60 P. "IS ALLOWED FOR CUMULATIVE TIME.":P.:P.
 80 IN. "HOW MANY ENEMIES DO YOU WISH TO TAKE ON ";M
 85 O=0:CLS
 90 H=0
100 FOR Y=0 TO 38:X=63:SET(X,Y):N. Y
110 FOR Y=12 TO 14:X=63:RESET(X,Y):N. Y
120 FOR Y=0 TO 38:X=62:SET(X,Y):N.Y
130 FOR Y=12 TO 14:X=62:RESET(X,Y):N. Y
140 FOR X=0 TO 127:Y=38:SET(X,Y):N. X
160 G. 400
200 P.AT832,"PRESS ENTER TO FIRE LASER";:IN. A$
300 A=37:B=38:C=87
310 SET(B,A):SET(C,A)
320 IF B=62 G.500
330 A=A-1:B=B+1:C=C-1
340 G. 310
400 R=256+RND(62)
410 P.ATR,"*"
420 P.AT872,"TIME-----";H:P.AT896,"HITS---";O:P.AT930,"TO GO---";M-O
421 P.AT832,"HOW MANY DEGREES        ";:IN. F
422 IF F=0 G. 200
425 IF (R+F<=319)*(R+F>=256) G. 430
427 P.AT1020,"OUT OF RANGE AT ";F;" DEGREES":G. 420
430 R=R+F
440 P.ATR-F," ":P.ATR,"*"
450 H=H+: IF H=M*3 G. 600
460 G. 420
500 IF R=287 G. 550
510 CLS:P. "MISS":G. 590
550 CLS:P. "KA-BAM! YOU GOT 'EM ACE!"
560 O=O+1:IF O=M G. 700
590 H=H+1:IF H=M*3 G. 600
595 IN. "PRESS ENTER TO CONTINUE";A$:CLS:G. 100
600 CLS:P. "TIME'S UP. YOU ONLY DESTROYED ";O;" OF THE ";M
610 P. "POSSIBLE ENEMIES FOR A RATING OF ";O/M*100;"%"
620 END
700 CLS:P. "HURRAY! YOU GOT 'EM ALL WITH TIME TO SPARE!"
710 END
```

Flying Fortress

Player tries to hit a horizontal target by instructing his plane when to drop it's bomb. See Fig. 6-10.

Variable List

D - Number of rounds to be played
J - Round number.
U, V - Used is drawing target.
E, F, A, B, G, H - Used in drawing plane.
R - Elapsed seconds.
S - When to release bomb.
I, O - Used to plot movement of bomb.
K - Number of targets hit by player.

Suggested Variations

■ Examine the message printing routine. Can you apply this to other programs in this chapter?
■ Change the size of the target from turn to turn.
■ Change the altitude of the plane from turn to turn.

Program Listing

```
  5 CLS:P.:P.:P."FLYING FORTRESS":P.
 10 P. "IN THIS GAME, YOU MUST INSTRUCT YOUR PLANE WHEN TO"
 15 K=0
 20 P. "DROP IT'S BOMB IN ORDER TO HIT THE ENEMY'S FUEL DUMP."
 30 IN. "HOW MANY ROUNDS DO YOU WISH TO PLAY ";D
 32 CLS
 35 FOR J=1 TO D
 40 P.AT64,"ROUND #";J
100 U=47:V=RND(119):IF V<40 G. 100
102 R=V+8
105 FOR Z=V TO R
106 SET(Z,U)
110 N. Z
150 E=5:F=16:SET(E,F)
160 B=17
170 FOR A=0 TO 7
180 SET(A,B)
190 N. A
192 A=A–1
195 G=5:H=18:SET(G,H)
```

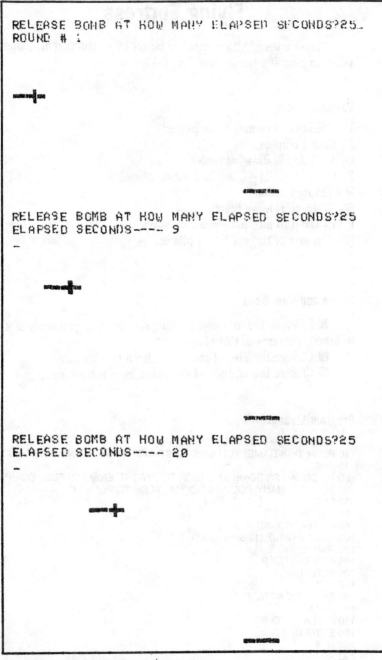

RELEASE BOMB AT HOW MANY ELAPSED SECONDS?25
ROUND # 1

RELEASE BOMB AT HOW MANY ELAPSED SECONDS?25
ELAPSED SECONDS---- 9

RELEASE BOMB AT HOW MANY ELAPSED SECONDS?25
ELAPSED SECONDS---- 20

Fig. 6-10. Example of the Flying Fortress program.

118

```
RELEASE BOMB AT HOW MANY ELAPSED SECONDS?25
ELAPSED SECONDS---- 30
```

```
RELEASE BOMB AT HOW MANY ELAPSED SECONDS?25
ELAPSED SECONDS---- 43
```

```
RELEASE BOMB AT HOW MANY ELAPSED SECONDS?25
ELAPSED SECONDS---- 52
```

```
PRESS ENTER TO CONTINUE?_
```

```
BOY O BOY! WHAT A PILOT!
```

```
197 G. 300
200 E=E+1:A=A+1
202 R=R+1
203 P.AT64,"ELAPSED SECONDS----";R
205 G=G+1
210 SET(E,F)SET(A,B):SET(G,H)
220 RESET(E-1,F)
222 IF A=8 THEN RESET(A-8,B)
224 IF A>8 THEN RESET(A-9,B)
226 RESET(G-1,H)
228 IF R>=S G. 350
230 G. 200
300 P.AT0,"RELEASE BOMB AT HOW MANY ELAPSED SECONDS";:
    IN. S
303 T=0
305 R=0:G. 200
350 IF T=1 G. 360
355 T=1:I=G:O=H
360 I=I+1: O=O+1
370 SET(I,O):RESET(I-1,O-1)
380 IF POINT(I+1,O+1)=1 G. 500
390 IF O>=47 G. 550
400 G. 200
500 P=RND(5):ON P GOS. 1000,1010,1020,1030,1040
510 P.AT192,"PRESS ENTER TO CONTINUE";:IN. A$
515 CLS
520 K=K+1:G. 600
550 P=RND(5):ON P GOS. 1050, 1060, 1070, 1080, 1090
555 P.AT192,"PRESS ENTER TO CONTINUE";:IN. A$
560 CLS:G. 600
600 N. J
605 CLS
610 P. "YOU HIT ";K;" TARGETS OUT OF ";J-1
620 P. "FOR A SCORE OF ";K/(J-1)*100;"%"
630 END
1000 P.AT900,"YAARGH! YOU GOT ME!"
1005 RETURN
1010 P.AT900, "SAY, DID YOU FLY IN W. W. II?"
1015 RETURN
1020 P.AT900,"THINK YOU'RE SMART, DON'T YOU?"
1025 RETURN
1030 P.AT900,"OUCH! WHAT A REVOLTING DEVELOPMENT!"
1035 RETURN
1040 P.AT900,"HEY! CUT THAT OUT!"
1045 RETURN
1050 P.AT900,"ARK! ARK! ARK! WHAT A LOUSY SHOT!"
1055RETURN
1060 P.AT900,"HOOO BOY!  YOU MUST BE BLIND!"
1065 RETURN
1070 P.AT900,"MISSED ME, MISSED ME, NOW YOU GOTTA KISS ME!"
1075 RETURN
1080 P.AT900,"NICE TRY, SUCKER."
1085 RETURN
1090 P.AT900,"JEEZ, DON'T YOU EVER GIVE UP?"
1095 RETURN
```

120

Supermaze

Player tries to maneuver his man through a maze while avoiding all Ss (supermazes) and Ms (mines).

Variable Listing

A - Position of player's man.
T - Direction of movement (status)
R - Direction of movement entered from keyboard.
A(U) - Position of mines: A(1) to A(100).
A(T+100) - Position of supermazes: A(101) to A(200).

Suggested Variations

■ Add a command that can be used a limited number of times to place the player elsewhere in the maze randomly.
■ To increase the difficulty, add more mines and supermazes. Be careful to keep your array locations separated.

Program Listing

```
 5 CLS:P.:P.:P."SUPERMAZE":P.
10 P. "THE OBJECT OF THIS GAME IS TO MANEUVER";
15 P. "YOUR MAN (THE *)"
20 P. "THROUGH THE MAZE TO THE RIGHT EDGE OF THE SCREEN. HITTING"
30.P. "A MINE (M) WILL DESTROY YOU. HITTING A SUPERMAZE (S) WILL"
40 P. "CAUSE A NEW MAZE TO BE PRINTED, MAYBE DROPPING A MINE ON"
50 P. "YOU! STEER AS FAR AWAY FROM ALL S'S AND M'S AS POSSIBLE"
55 P. "BECAUSE NOT ALL MINES AND SUPERMAZES ARE VISBLE."
60 P. "DIRECTIONS OF MOVEMENT ARE:"
62 P. "         1    2"
64 P. "          *    3"
66 P. "        5    4      ";
67 P. "ENTERING 6 WILL CAUSE THE MAZE TO"
68 P.              BE REPRINTED."
70 T=0:P.:IN. "PRESS ENTER TO START GAME";A$:CLS
80 CLS
85 GOS. 200
87 GOS. 400
90 A=512
100 FOR X=0 TO 127:Y=38:SET(X,Y):N. X
110 REM *** POSITION PRINT
115 IF T=1 THEN P.ATA+64," ";
116 IF T=2 THEN P.ATA+63," "
117 IF T=3 THEN P.ATA-1," "
118 IF T=4 THEN P.ATA-65," "
```

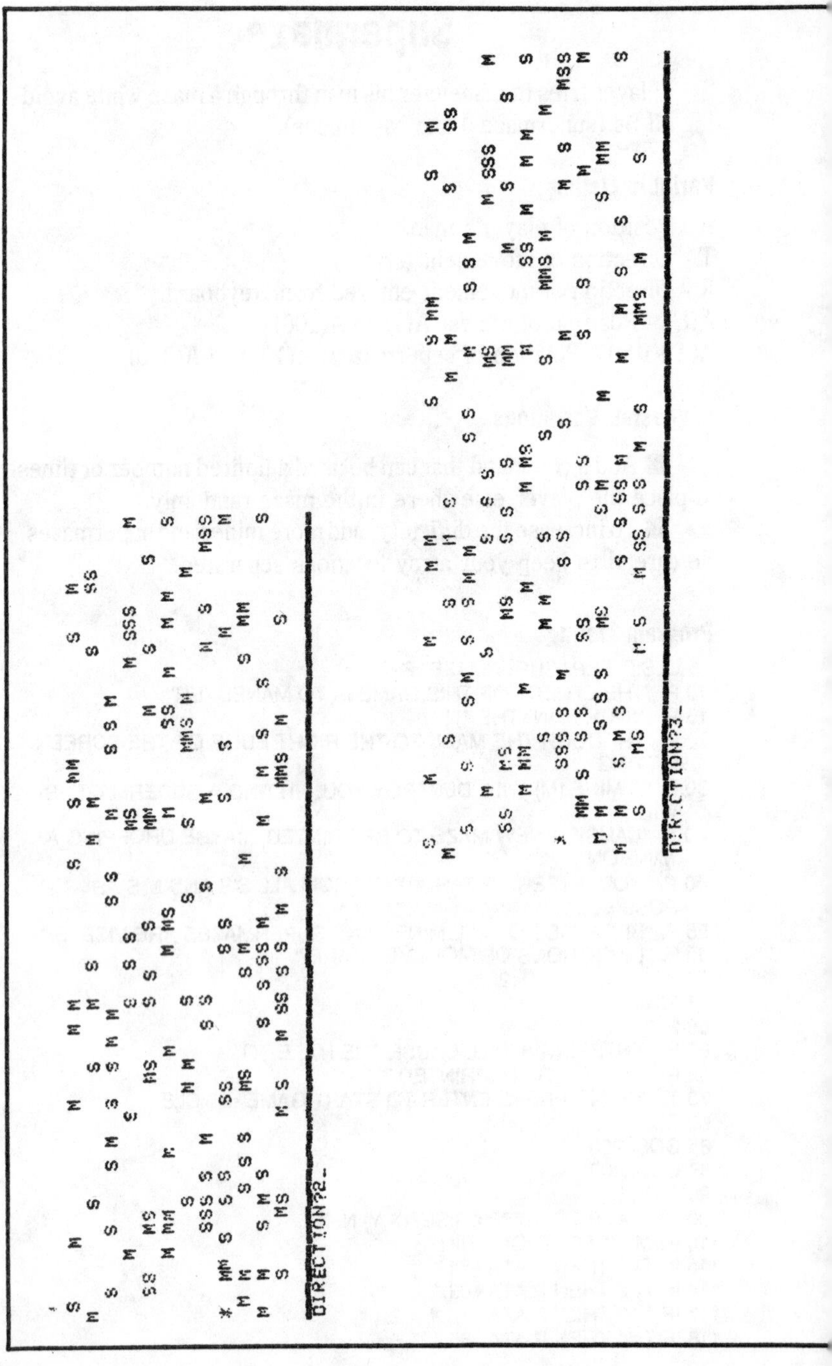
DIRECTION?2_
DIRECTION?3_

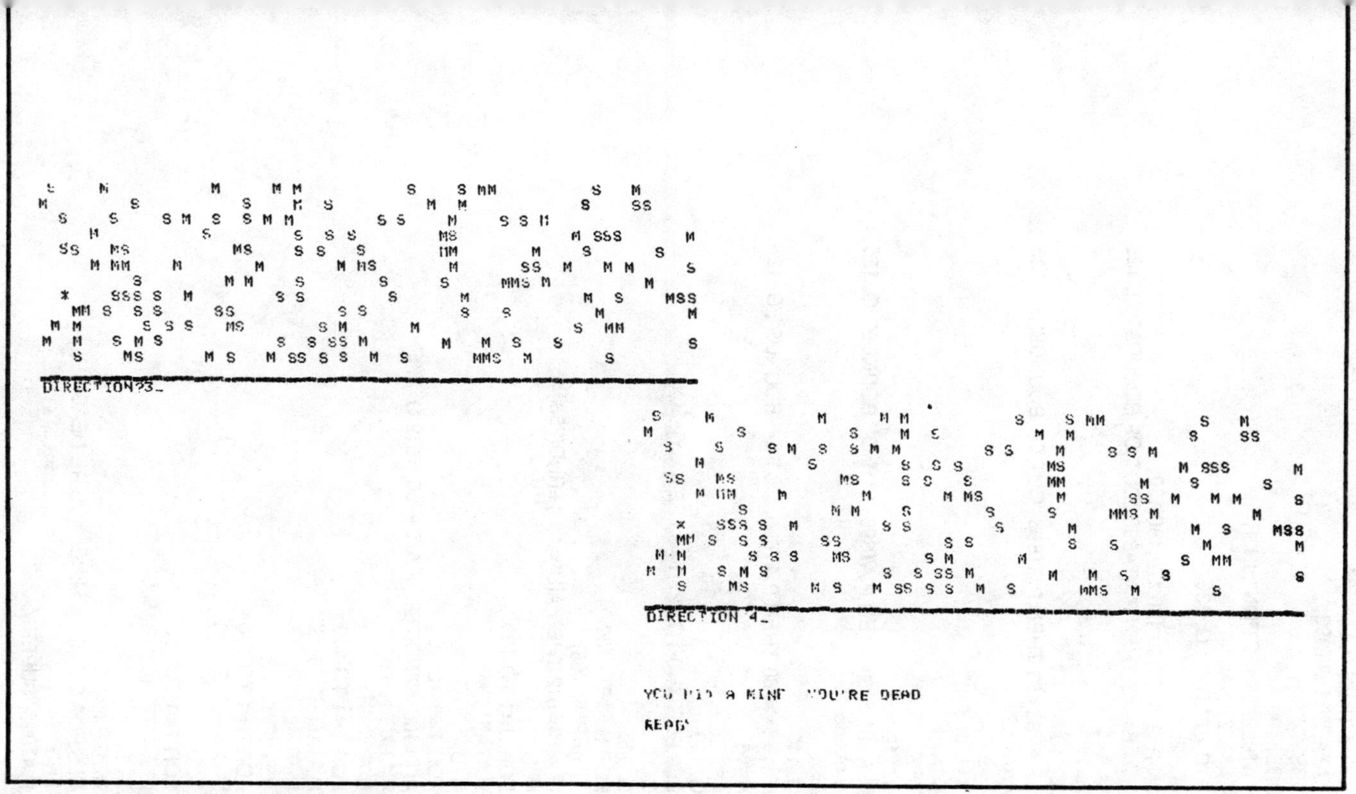

Fig. 6-11. Example of the Supermaze.

```
119 IF T=5 THEN P.ATA-64," "
120 P.ATA,"*";:P.AT896,"          ";
122 GOS. 700
123 GOS. 400
125 P.AT832,"DIRECTION";:IN. R
127 P.AT832,"WAIT . . . . . . . . ."
128 IF (R>0)*(R<7) G. 130
129. G. 125
130 ON R G. 140,150,160,170,180,190
140 IF A-64<63 THEN P.ATA896,"OUT OF BOUNDS";:G. 125
142 A=A-64
144 T=1
145 G. 110
150 OF A-63<63 THEN P.AT896,"OUT OF BOUNDS";:G. 125
153 A=A-63
154 T=2
155 G. 110
160 A=A=1
164 T=3
165 G. 110
170 IF A+65>768 THEN P.AT896,"OUT OF BOUNDS";:G. 125
172 A=A+65
174 T=4
175 G. 110
180 IF A+64>768 THEN P.AT896,"OUT OF BOUNDS";:G. 125
182 A=64
184 T=5
185 G. 110
190 CLS:FOR X=0 TO 127:Y=38:SET(X,Y);:N.X
192 GOS. 230
195 G. 110
200 FOR U=1 TO 100
210 A(U)=RND(768)
215 IF A(U)=512 THEN A(U)=A(U)+RND(256)
220 N. U
230 FOR U=1 TO 100
240 P.ATA(U),"M";
250 N. U
270 FOR T=1 TO 100
275 A(T+100)=RND(768):IF A(T+100)=512 G. 275
277 P.ATA(T+100),"S";
280 N. T
290 FOR T=1 TO 100
300 P.ATA(T+100),"S";
310 N. T
320 RETURN
400 FOR U=1 TO 100
410 IF A=A(U) G. 500
420 N. U
430 FOR T=1 TO 100
440 IF A=A(T+100) G. 600
450 N. T
460 RETURN
500 CLS:P. "YOU HIT A MINE! YOU'RE DEAD!"
510 END
600 P.AT896,"SUPERMAZE!";
```

124

```
610 FOR Z=1 TO 1000:N. Z
620 CLS:GOS. 200
630 G. 100
700 IF (A=63)+(A=127)+(A=191)+(A=255)+(A=319) G. 800
710 IF (A=383)+(A=447)+(A=511)+(A=575)+(A=639) G. 800
720 IF (A=703)+(A=767) G. 800
730 RETURN
800 CLS:P. "YOU'VE MADE IT!!! YOU WIN!!"
810 END
```

Chapter 7
Home and Business
Application Programs

Many microcomputer owners will wish to use their system to aid them in household chores such as filekeeping and calculation. The programs in this chapter will aid the average homeowner or small business or manufacturer in many of these operations.

Although many business programs must be suited to the particular needs of that business, all efforts have been made to keep these programs as universally adaptable as possible. When modification for use must be made, such as in the program SIMPLE INVENTORY, all documentation needed for modification is included.

I have tried to keep all of these programs on a level where they will be interesting to run and examine even for users who have no business need for them.

One final note: the program LOAN PAYMENT will *not* give an indication of the true amount that will be charged for each loan payment. The average payment amount given is just that, the amount of money that will ultimately be paid to the loaner divided by the number of payments. You should discuss this with your loaner to obtain the true payment schedule.

Executive Decision Maker

Anyone can flip a coin. It takes a real executive to use an Executive Decision Maker. Or at least an armchair executive.

Variable List

A$ - First option.
B$ - Second option.

Z - Time delay loop.
A - Used to seed RND generator.
C - Decides which order to print YES and NO.
B - Loop of 1 to A

Suggested Variations

■ This program is made for jazzing up. Use your imagination and butcher away!

■ Add a function so that more than two options may be listed.

Sample Run

```
ENTER YOUR FIRST OPTION (UP TO 16 CHARACTERS INCLUDING
    SPACES)?EAT WORMS
ENTER YOUR SECOND OPTION?EAT DIRT
```

```
THE DECISION IS:

EAT WORMS                                           EAT DIRT

YES                                                      NO
```

```
THE DECISION IS:
EAT WORMS                                           EAT DIRT
YES                                                      NO
    DON'T BECOME ANOTHER J. WILLIAMS! THE DECISION IS FINAL.
```

Program Listing

```
1 CLS P. ##########################################"
3 P.
4 P.
5 P.
6 P ' EXECUTIVE DECISION MAKER"
7 P.
8 P.
9 P.
10 P "##########################################"
11 FOR Z=1 TO 1500:N. Z:CLS
12 P. "J. WILLIAMS OF 5TH AVE., NEW YORK CITY, DID NOT LISTEN"
20 P. "TO THE ADVICE OF HIS EXECUTIVE DECISION MAKER BEFORE"
25 P. "MAKING AN IMPORTANT INVESTMENT..."
30 FOR Z=1 TO 4000:N. Z:CLS
40 P. "J. WILLIAMS IS NOW A RETAIL PENCIL SALESMAN ON A"
50 P. "STREET CORNER IN EAST ST. LOUIS."
55 FOR Z=1 TO 2000:N. Z:CLS
60 FOR X=1 TO 5:CLS:FOR Z=1 TO 250:N. Z
61 P.AT532, "THINK ABOUT IT";for Z=1 TO 250:N,Z:N,X
65     CLS
150 P. "ENTER YOUR FIRST OPTION (UP TO 16 CHARACTERS)";A$
155 IN "ENTER YOUR SECOND OPTION ";B$
```

```
160 CLS
200 A=RND(100):IF A<=20 G. 200
210 FOR B=1 TO A
220 CLS:P"THE DECISION IS:"

222 P.:P.
223 P.TAB(4),A$,TAB(44),B$
225 C=RND(2)
230 IF C=1 G. 500
240 G. 600
250 N. B
260 G. 800
500 P.
510 P.TAB(7),"YES",TAB(47),"YES"
520 G. 250
600 P.
610 P.TAB(7),"NO",TAB(47),"YES"
611 G. 250
800 P.
810 P. "THE DECISION IS FINAL."
812 P.:P. 'DON'T BECOME ANOTHER J. WILLIAMS!"
815 END
```

An Expensive Timepiece

What? You paid all of that money for a computer and when you're not using it is sits there like a paper weight? Well, here's a program that turns it into an expensive clock!NOTE: This clock will only be as accurate as you make it. The loop in Line #90 will need to be calibrated to your particular system. A larger parameter will slow down the clock, and a smaller will speed it up. See Fig. 7-1.

Variable List

H - Hours.
M - Minutes.
S - Seconds.
N - 1 second delay timer.

Suggested Variations

Change this program to read as a 24 hour clock.
Change this program to print messages (Cuckoo?) at various times.

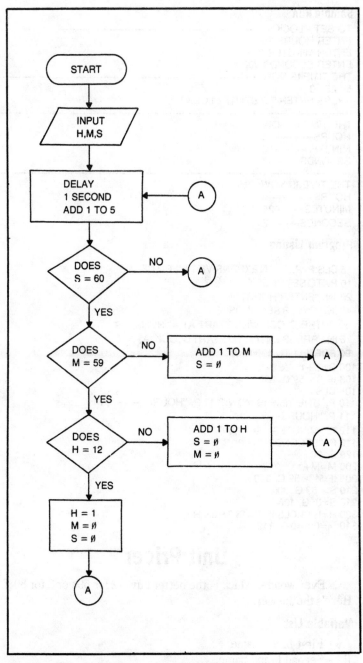

Fig. 7-1. Flowchart for the Expensive Timepiece.

Sample Run

```
TO SET CLOCK -----------------------------------------------------------------
ENTER HOURS ?5
ENTER MINUTES ?25
ENTER SECONDS ?00
THE TIME IS NOW -------------------------------------------------------------
5 : 25 : 0
PRESS ENTER TO START CLOCK?
-----------------------------------------------------------------------------
THE TIME IS NOW:
  HOURS------------ 5
  MINUTES--------- 25
  SECONDS ---------1
-----------------------------------------------------------------------------
THE TIME IS NOW:
  HOURS ------------5
  MINUTES---------25
  SECONDS---------2
```

Program Listing

```
  5 CLS:P.:P.:P."AN EXPENSIVE TIMEPIECE":P..
 10 P."TO SET CLOCK---"
 20 IN. "ENTER HOURS*";H
 40 IN. "ENTER SECONDS";S
 60 P."THE CLOCK WILL START AT---";H;":";M;":";S
 70 IN. "PRESS ENTER TO START CLOCK"A$
 90 FORN=1 TO 470:N. N
100 S=S+1
103 IF S> 59 G. 200
105 CLS
110 P. "THE TIME IS NOW:"111 P. "HOURS-------- ";H
111 P. "HOURS-------- ";H
112 P. "MINUTES-------- ";M
113 P. "SECONDS-------- ";S
120 G. 90
200 M=M+1
203 IF M > 59 G. 300
210 S> 59 G. 300
210 S=0: G. 105
300 H=H+1:CLS:IF H=13 THEN H=1
310 M=0:S=0:G. 110
```

Unit Pricer

Ever wonder which is the better buy—2 for 59¢ or 3 for 80¢?
Here's the answer.

Variable List

A$ - First brand name.
B$ - Second brand name.
A - Cost of A$.

B - How many units of A$.

C - Cost of B$.

D - How many units of B$.

E - Unit price of A$.

F - Unit price of B$.

Suggested Variations

■ Change program to accommodate more than two items at a time.

■ Calculate and display units per cent (or per dollar).

Sample Run

WHAT IS THE BRAND NAME OF THE FIRST PRODUCT? SCUM-WELL'S
HOW MUCH DOES THIS PACKAGE OF SCUMWELL'S SELL FOR?2.95
HOW MANY UNITS (OUNCES GRAMS, ETC.) IN THIS PACKAGE?15
WHAT IS THE BRAND NAME OF THE SECOND PRO-DUCT?POOBAH'S
HOW MANY UNITS. 9
SCUMWELL'S-----19.6667 CENTS PER UNIT.
POOBAH'S-----16.8889 CENTS PER UNIT.
POOBAH's IS THE BETTER BUY ACCORDING TO UNIT PRICE
NEED PROGRAM AGAIN (1=YES 2=NO)?2

Program Listing

```
  5 CLS:P.:P.:P."UNIT PRICER":P.
 10 P. "THIS PROGRAM COMPARES TWO GROCERY PRODUCTS FOR
    THE"
 20 P. "BEST BUY"BASED ON THEIR UNIT PRICE. UNITS MUST
 30 P. "BE CONSISTANT FOR BOTH ITEMS FOR BEST EVALUATION--"
 35 P. "(OUNCES, GRAMS, ETC.)"
 50 P.:P.:IN. "WHAT IS THE BRAND NAME OF THE FIRST PRODUCT";A$
 60 P. "HOW MUCH DOES THIS PACKAGE OF";A$;" COST";:IN. A
 70 IN. "HOW MANY UNITS IN THIS PACKAGE (OUNCES, GRAMS,
    ETC.)";B
 80 IN. "WHAT IS THE BRAND NAME OF THE SECOND PRODUCT ";B$
 90 IN. "WHAT IS THE PRICE";C
100 IN. "HOW MANY UNITS ";D
110 CLS:P.:P.:E=A/B:F=C/D:E=E*100:F=F*100
120 P. A$;"--------";E;" CENTS PER UNIT."
130 P. B$;"--------";F;" CENTS PER UNIT."
140 IF E < F G. 150
142 IF E=F G. 200
145 P. B$;" IS THE BETTER BUY ACCORDING TO UNIT PRICE."
147 G. 250
150 P. A$;" IS THE BETTER BUY ACCORDING TO UNIT PRICE."
155 G. 250
200 P. 'BOTH ";A$;" AND ";B$;" ARE EQUALLY PRICED."
250 IN. "NEED PROGRAM AGAIN (1=YES 2=NO) ";X
255 IF X=1 G. 50
260 END
```

Metric Converter

These are some of the most popular metric and U.S. Conversions. This program can save a heck of a lot of time on a variety of applications.

Variable List

U - Menu choice.
A - Conversion choice.
B - How many units.
A$,B$ -contains abbreviations of metric and U. S. units.
C - conversion of B for choice A.

Suggested Variations

■ This one's wide open. Add as many useful conversions as you need and your memory allows.

Sample Run

```
ENTER 1 FOR METRIC TO ENGLISH OR 2 FOR ENGLISH TO METRIC?2
 8) INCHES TO CENTIMETERS
 9) YARDS TO METERS
10) CUBIC INCHES TO CUBIC CENTIMETERS
11) MILES TO KILOMETERS
12) GALLONS TO LITERS
13) OUNCES TO GRAMS
14) POUNDS TO KILOGRAMS
15) DEGREES F. TO DEGREES C.
16) DEGREES C. TO DEGREES F.
ENTER YOUR CHOICE NUMBER (1 TO 16)?12..........................................
--------------------------------------------------------------------------------
HOW MANY GAL
75
5 GAL = 18.926 L
--------------------------------------------------------------------------------
TYPE 1 TO CONTINUE OR 2 to QUIT?2
```

Program Listing

```
1 CLS:P.:P.:P."METRIC CONVERTER":P.
2 IN."ENTER 1 FOR METRIC TO U.S. OR 2 FOR U.S. TO METRIC";U
3 CLS:ON U G. 20, 90
20 P. "1) CENTIMETERS TO INCHES"
30 P. "2) METERS TO YARDS"
40 P. "3) CUBIC CENTIMETERS TO CUBIC INCHES"
50 P. "4) KILOMETERS TO MILES"
60 P. "5) LITERS TO GALLONS"
70 P. "6) GRAMS TO OUNCES"
80 P. "7) KILOGRAMS TO POUNDS"
85 G. 180
90 P. "8) INCHES TO CENTIMETERS"
100 P. "9) YARDS TO METERS"
```

```
110 P. "10) CUBIC INCHES TO CUBIC CENTIMETERS"
120 P. "11) MILES TO KILOMETERS"
130 P. "12) GALLONS TO LITERS"
140 P. "13) OUNCES TO GRAMS"
150 P. "14) POUNDS TO KILOGRAMS"
160 P. "15) DEGREES F. TO DEGREES C."
170 P. "16) DEGREES C. TO DEGREES F."
180 IN. "ENTER YOUR CHOICE NUMBER (1 TO 16)";A
190 IF (A< =1)*(A < =16) G.200
195 P. "BAD CHOICE NUMBER":G. 180
200 A=INT(A)
210 P."-----------------------------------------------------------------------"
220 IF A=1 THEN A$="CM":B$="IN"
230 IF A=2 THEN A$="M":B$="YDS"
240 IF A=3 THEN A$="CC":B$="CI"
250 IF A=4 THEN A$="KM":B$="MI"
260 IF A=5 THEN A$="L":B$="GAL"
270 IF A=6 THEN A$="G":B$="OZ"
280 IF A=7 THEN A$="KG":B$="LBS"
290 IF A=8 THEN A$="IN":B$="CM"
300 IF A=9 THEN A$="YDS":B$="M"
310 IF A=10 THEN A$="CI":B$="CC"
320 IF A=11 THEN A$="MI":B$="KM"
330 IF A=12 THEN A$="GAL":$="L"
340 IF A=13 THEN A$="OZ":B$="G"
350 IF A=14 THEN A$="LBS":B$="KG"
360 IF A=15 THEN A$="DEG. F.":B$="DEG. C"
370 IF A=16 THEN A$="DEG. C.":B$="DEG. F"
380 P. "HOW MANY ";A$:IN. B.
400 IF A=1 THEN C=B*.3937
410 IF A=2 THEN C=B*1.0936
420 IF A=3 THEN C=B*.061025
430 IF A=4 THEN C=B*.621377
440 IF A=5 THEN C=B*.26418
450 IF A=6 THEN C=B*.03527
460 IF A=7 THEN C=B*2.02046
470 IF A=8 THEN C=B*2.54
480 IF A=9 THEN C=B*.91441
490 IF A=10 THEN C=B*1.6386
500 IF A=11 THEN C=B*1.6093
510 IF A=12 THEN C=B*3.7852
520 IF A=13 THEN C=B*28.3527
530 IF A=14 THEN C=B*.49493
540 IF A=15 THENC=(B-32)*(5/9)
550 IF A=16 THEN C=B*(9/5)+32
560 P.
570 P. B;" ";A$;" = ";C;" ";B$
590 IN. 'TYPE 1 TO CONTINUE OR 2 TO QUIT ;V
600 IF V=1 G. 2
610
```

Salary Evaluator

You'll be suprised about how much you don't know about your paycheck! Don't let the shortness of this program fool you, it's packed with provocative information. See Fig. 7-2.

Variable List

A - Total hours worked in pay period.
B - Gross earnings before tax.
C - Amount deducted.
D - Total earnings per hour.
F - Actual take home per hour.
G - Amount deducted per hour.
H - percent of gross earnings deducted.

Suggested Variations

■ Whatever you want to know about your paycheck is at your fingertips . . . use your imaginations!

■ Write an addition to create a tape file for your paychecks.

Sample Run

```
ENTER TOTAL HOURS WORKED IN THIS PAY PERIOD?40
ENTER TOTAL EARNINGS BEFORE TAX AND OTHER DEDUCTIONS?
  245
ENTER TOTAL AMOUNT DEDUCTED AS TAX AND OTHER ASSESS-
  MENT?85  SALARY EVALUATION
--------------------------------------------------------------------------------------
  TOTAL EARNINGS PER HOUR---$ 6.125
  ACTUAL TAKE HOME PER HOUR-$ 4
  AMOUNT DEDUCTED PER HOUR--$ 2.125
  --------------------------------
  34.6939 % OF YOUR EARNINGS WAS DEDUCTED
```

Program Listing

```
  5 CLS:P.:P.:P."SALARY EVALUATOR";p.
 10 IN. "ENTER TOTAL HOURS WORKED IN THIS PAY PERIOD";A
 20 IN. "ENTER TOTAL EARNINGS BEFORE TAX AND OTHER
      DEDUCTIONS";B
 30 IN. "ENTER TOTAL AMOUNT DEDUCTED AS TAX AND OTHER
      ASSESSMENTS";C
 40 CLS:P. "SALARY EVALUATION"
 50 P. " -----------------------------------------------------------------------------------"
 60 D=B/A:E=B-C:F=E/A:G=C/A:H=C*100/B
 70 P. "TOTAL EARNINGS PER HOUR— $";D
 80 P."ACTUAL TAKE HOME PER HOUR- $";F
 90 P."AMOUNT DEDUCTED PER HOUR— $";G
105 P.:P. H;"% OF YOUR EARNINGS WAS DEDUCTED"
110 END
```

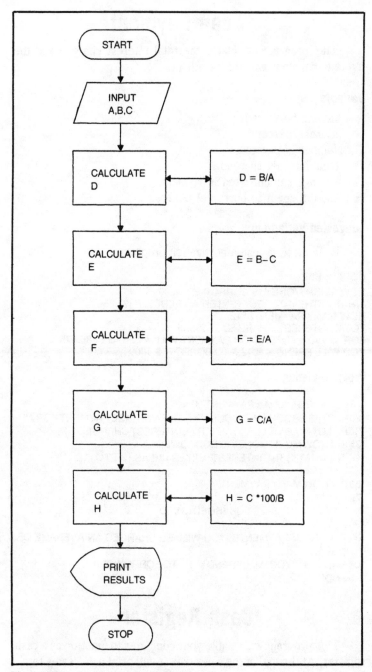

Fig. 7-2. Flowchart for the Salary Evaluator.

Loan Payment

This program calculates the total interest charged and the average payment amount for a loan.

Variable List

A - Amount borrowed.
B - Interest (percent).
C - Number of payments.
D - Total interest charged.
G - Average amount of each payment.
H - Amount spent to borrow A dollars.

Suggested Variations

■ Work up a loan amortization program.

Sample Run

```
HOW MUCH MONEY IS BORROWED?1000
WHAT IS THE INTEREST (ENTER AS PERCENT)?4.25
HOW MANY PAYMENTS?12
TOTAL INTEREST CHARGED IS $ 42.5
FOR 12 PAYMENTS, EACH PAYMENT WILL AVERAGE $86.875
YOU WILL SPEND $ 1042.5 TO BORROW $ 1000
```

Program Listing

```
  5 CLS:P.:P.:P. "LOAN PAYMENT":P.
 20 P. "THIS PROGRAM CALCULATES THE AVERAGE PAYMENT FOR A"
 30 P. "LOAN, AS WELL AS THE TOTAL INTEREST CHARGED.":P.
 35 IN. "HOW MUCH MONEY IS BORROWED";A
 40 IN. "WHAT IS THE INTEREST (ENTER 13% AS 13, ETC.)";B
 50 B=B/100
 60 IN. "HOW MANY PAYMENTS";C
 70 D=A*B
 80 P. "TOTAL INTEREST CHARGED IS $";D
 90 E=D/C:F=A/C:G=F+E
100 P."FOR";C;"PAYMENTS, YOU WILL BE CHARGED AN AVERAGE OF
    $";G
105 H=D+A:P. "YOU WILL SPEND $";H;"TO BORROW $";A
110 END
```

Cash Register

This program will enable your computer to function as a cash register. At the end of the sales day, it will print a   sales total. See Fig. 7-3.

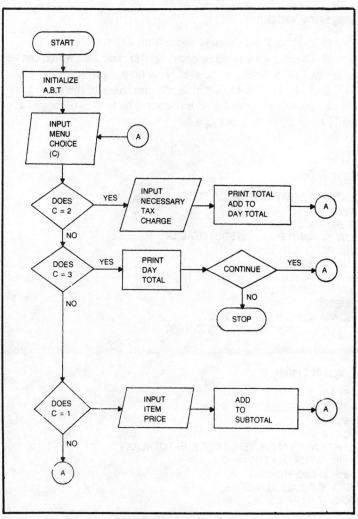

Fig. 7-3. Flowchart for the Cash Register.

Variable List

C - Menu choice.
P - Item price.
A - Running subtotal.
B - Tax on $A
D - Purchase total.
T - Day total.

Suggested Variations

■ Print day tax charged along with day total.

■ There are many other cash register functions which can be added to this program as needed. Just dive right in!

■ Add a system so that multiple purchases of the same price can be entered in one entry. For instance, forty bars of soap at 49c could be entered as .49,40.

Sample Run

```
ENTER 1 FOR ITEM, 2 FOR SUBTOTAL, OR
3 FOR DAY TOTAL? 1
ITEM PRICE? 1.48
ENTR 1 FOR ITEM, 2 FOR SUBTOTAL, OR
3 FOR DAY TOTAL?1
ITEM PRICE?2.56
ENTER 1 FOR ITEM, 2 FOR SUBTOTAL, OR
3 FOR DAY TOTAL?2
SUBTOTAL------$4.04
HOW MUCH TAX ON $4.04 ?.20
PRESS ENTER FOR NEXT CUSTOMER?
```

Program Listing

```
  5 CLS
 10 P. "CASH REGISTER"P.:P.
 15 T=0
 20 A=0:B=0
 30 P. "ENTER 1 FOR ITEM, 2 FOR SUB-TOTAL, OR"
 40 IN. "3 FOR DAY TOTAL";C
 45 IF (C<=0)+(C<3) G. 30
 50 ON C G.100,200,400
100 IN. ITEM PRICE";P
110 A=A+P
120 G. 30
200 P. "SUBTOTAL------$";A
210 P.:P. "HOW MUCH TAX ON $";A;
220 IN.B
300 P.
310 D=A+B
320 T=T+D
330 P. "PURCHASE TOTAL-----$";D
340 IN. "PRESS ENTER FOR NEXT CUSTOMER";A$
345 CLS
350 G.20
400 P. "DAY TOTAL-------$";T
```

138

450 IN. "ENTER 1 TO CONTINUE DAY, OR 2 TO DISCONTINUE";P
460 IF P=1 G. 20
470 END

Calendar Calculators

This is a useful program to find out what day of the week a certain date falls on, or fell on in the past. Just remember that the date must be after the change to the present calendar system (1752).

Variable List

M - Month of specified date.
D - Day of specified date.
Y - Year of specified date.
Z - Calculated day of the week.

Suggested Variations

■ Write a menu of holidays, such as Christmas and Fourth of July, that can be assessed immediately after the desired year is entered.

Sample Run

```
DATE MUST BE ACCORDING TO CURRENT CALENDAR
SYSTEM TO BE CORRECT.
ENTER MONTH, DAY, YEAR (EX. 5,21,1979) ?7,2,79
ENTER MONTH, DAY, YEAR (EX. 5,21,1979) ?7,2,1979
JULY 2, 1979 IS A MONDAY
```

Program Listing

```
  5 CLS:P.:P.:P."CALENDAR CALCULATOR":P.
 10 P. "DATE MUST BE ACCORDING TO CURRENT CALENDAR"
 20 P. "SYSTEM TO BE CORRECT."
 30 IN. "ENTER MONTH, DAY, YEAR (EX. 5, 21, 1979) ";M,D,Y
 35 IF Y<1753 THEN P. "ERROR";CLS;G. 10
 40 K=INT(.6+(1/M))
 50 L=Y-K
 60 0=M+12*K
 70 P=L/100
 80 A=INT(P/4)
 90 B=INT(P)
100 C=INT((5*L)/4)
110 E=INT(13*(0+1)/5)
120 Z=E+C-B+A+D-1
130 Z=(Z-(7*INT(Z/7)))+1
140 IF M=1 THEN P. "JANUARY";
150 IF M=2 THEN P. "FEBRUARY";
```

```
160 IF M=3 THEN P. "MARCH";
170 IF M=4 THEN P. "APRIL";
180 IF M=5 THEN P. "MAY";
190 IF M=6 THEN P. "JUNE";
200 IF M=7 THEN P. "JULY";
210 IF M=8 THEN P. "AUGUST";
220 IF M =9 THEN P. "SEPTEMBER";
230 IF M=10 THEN P. "OCTOBER";
240 IF M=11 THEN P. "NOVEMBER";
250 IF M=12 THEN P. "DECEMBER";
260 P. D;", ";Y;" IS A ";
270 IF Z=1 THEN P. "SUNDAY."
280 IF Z=2 THEN P. "MONDAY."
290 IF Z=3 THEN P. "TUESDAY."
300 IF Z=4 THEN P. "WEDNESDAY."
310 IF Z=5 THEN P. "THURSDAY."
320 IF Z=6 THEN P. "FRIDAY."
330 IF Z=7 THEN P. "SATURDAY."
340 END
```

Checkbook Wizard

Here is a program which verifies and records bank statements to create a tape file. Remember to use the space bar to delete any graphic blocks which remain after typing in the check's recipient.

Variable List

Z - Menu choice.
A$ - Month.
D - Starting balance.
F - Running balance.
G - Number of checks.
N - Number of first check used.
H - Current check number.
B$ - Who check was written to.
C - Amount of check H.
J - Number of deposits.
K - Current deposit.
L - Amount of deposit K.
M - Service charges total.

Suggested Variations

■ Write an addition to accommodate other types of accounts, such as savings.

Sample Run

DO YOU WANT TO:

1) RECORD A MONTH FILE
2) PRINT A MONTH FILE
ENTER YOUR DESIRED CHOICE NUMBER?2
REWIND THE DATA TAPE OF DESIRED MONTH AND PLACE
THE RECORDER IN THE 'PLAY' MODE.
PRESS ENTER TO CONTINUE?

HOW MANY CHECKS?4
HOW MANY DEPOSITS?1

CHECK #	WRITTEN TO	AMOUNT	BALANCE
1	AL'S TAVERN	$ 15	$ 85
2	MASSAGE PARLOR	$ 25	$ 60
3	BEAUTY SHOP	$ 6.25	$ 53.75
4	DELTA CHI FRAT.	$ 2.5	$51.25
	DEPOSIT	$ 25	$ 76.25
	SERVICE CHARGE	$ 4.5	$ 71.75

FINAL BALANCE---- $ 71.75

Program Listing

```
   5 CLS:P.:P.:P."CHECKBOOK WIZARD":P.
  10 P. " DO YOU WAN TO;"
  20 P. "1)RECORD A MONTH FILE"
  30 P. "2) PRINT A MONTH FILE"
  40 IN. "ENTER YOUR CHOICE (1 OR 2)";Z
  50 IF Z=2G. 1000
  60 CLS
  70 IN. "WHAT MONTH IS THIS FOR";A$
  80 IN. "WHAT IS THE STARTING BALANCE";D
  85 F=D
  90 IN."HOW MANY CHECKS WERE USED";G
 100 IN. "WHAT IS THE NUMBER OF THE FIRST CHECK USED";N
 110 I=N+(G-1)
 120 P. "INSERT A FRESH CASSETTE INTO YOUR RECORDER AND
     REWIND"
 130 P."TO BEGINNING. PLACE RECORDER IN 'RECORD' MODE."
 140 IN. "PRESS ENTER WHEN READY";B$
 150 FOR H=N TO I
 155 CLS
 160 P.AT0,"CHECK #";H
 170 A=H
 180 P.AT256, "WHO WAS CHECK WRITTEN TO (USE SPACE BAR UNTIL"
 190 P.AT320,"GRAPHICS BLOCKS DISAPPEAR COMPLETELY";
 200 FOR X=73 TO 105:Y=16:SET(X,Y):N. X
 210 IN. B$
 230 P.AT384,"AMOUNT";:IN. C
 240 CLS:P. "PLEASE WAIT..."
 250 F=F- C
 260 PRINT # A;",";B$;",";C;",";F
 270 N. H
 280 IN. "HOW MANY DEPOSITS";J
 290 IF J=0 G. 400
 300 FOR K=1 TO J
 310 P. "DEPOSIT #";K;" WAS HOW MUCH";:IN. L.
```

141

```
320 CLS:P. "PLEASE WAIT..."
330 F=F+L
340 PRINT # L;",";F
350 N. K
400 IN. "HOW MUCH WAS THE TOTAL SERVICE CHARGES";M
410 CLS:F=F-M
420 PRINT # M;",";F
430 CLS
440 P. "TAPE RECORD FOR MONTH OF";A$;"IS COMPLETE."
450 P. "REMOVE CASSETTE AND RECORD THE FOLLOWING DATA"
460 P. "ON THE CASE:"
470 P. "MONTH----";A$
480 P. "CHECKS-----";G
500 P. "DEPOSITS---- ";J
505 P."STARTING BALANCE---- ";D
510 IN."PRESS ENTER TO CONTINUE"A$:CLS:G. 5
1000 P. "REWIND THE DATA TAPE OF DESIRED MONTH AND PLACE"
1010 P. "THE RECORDER IN THE 'PLAY' MODE."
1020 IN. "PRESS ENTER TO CONTINUE";B$
1030 CLS:IN. "HOW MANY CHECKS";0
1040 IN. "HOW MANY DEPOSITS ";P
1041 CLS:P.:P."CHECK #";TAB(10);"WRITTEN TO","AMOUNT",
     "BALANCE"
1042 FOR Q=1 TO 0
1045 INPUT # A,B$,C,F
1050    P. A;TAB(10) B$,"$";C,"$";F
1060 N. Q
1070 FOR R=1 TO P
1080 INPUT # C,F
1085 B$=DEPOSIT
1090 P.TAB(10);B$,"$";C,"$";F
1100 N. R
1110 INPUT # M,F
1115 B$=SERVICE CHARGE
1120 P.TAB(10);B$,"$";M,"$";F
1130 P. "FINAL BALANCE---- $";F
1140 END
```

Straight Line Depreciation

This program calculates depreciation data connected with the Straight Line method.

Variable List

(Input)

P - Purchase price of asset.

L - Life of asset.

D - Yearly depreciation (calculated).

Y - First year of use.

(Printout)

P - Current value at end of year Y.

142

Y - Current year.
Q - Year counter - exists program when Q=L

Suggested Variations

■ You might wish to include a reference column labeled *ORIGINAL PRICE*.

■ If you have the memory available, combine all three depreciation programs (Straight Line, Sum of the Years Digits, Double Declining Balance) to produce 1 strong depreciation program.

Sample Run

WHAT IS THE PURCHASE PRICE?25.00

WHAT IS THE ESTIMATED LIFETIME?2

DEPRECIATES $ 12.5 EACH YEAR
WHAT IS THE FIRST YEAR OF USE?1979

YEAR	VALUE
1979	$ 25
1980	$ 12.5

Program Listing

```
  1 CLS:P.:P.:P."STRAIGHT LINE DEPRECIATION":P.
  5 Q=0
 20 IN. "WHAT IS THE PURCHASE PRICE $";P
 25 IF P<=0 THEN P. "ERROR";G. 20
 30 CLS:IN. "WHAT IS THE ESTIMATED LIFE OF THE ASSET";L
 35 IF L<=0 THEN P. "ERROR":G. 30
 40 D=P/L
100 CLS:P. "DEPRECIATES $";D;" EACH YEAR."
110 P.:IN. "WHAT IS THE FIRST YEAR OF USE EX-1979 ";Y
120 CLS:P. "--------------------------------"
122 P. "YEAR","VALUE"
125 IF P<=0 G. 200
130 P. Y,"$";P
135 Q=Q+1: IF Q=10 G. 210
145 IF P<=0 G. 200
150 Y=Y+1:P=P-D
160 G. 125
200 END
210 IN. "PRESS ENTER TO CONTINUE";A$:CLS:Q=0:G. 145
```

Sum Of The Years Digits Depreciation

This program calculates depreciation data connected with the Sum of the Years Digits method.

Variable List

A - Price of asset. Later value of asset at end of year G.

B - Salvage value of asset.

D - Life of asset.

G - Year of use.

H - Yearly depreciation.

F - Remaining years of use. Exits program when F=0.

Suggested Variations

See Suggested Variations for Straight Line Depreciation.

Sample Run

```
ENTER THE PRICE (ROUNDED TO DOLLARS)?500
ENTER THE SALVAGE (OR TRADE IN) VALUE YOU EXPECT WHEN
YOU DISPOSE OF THIS ITEM (ROUNDED TO DOLLARS)? 150
ENTER THE NUMBER OF YEARS YOU EXPECT TO OWN THIS ITEM?9
WHAT IS THE FIRST YEAR OF USE--EX. 1979?1979
YEAR      DEPRECIATION     VALUE AT END OF YEAR
1979      $ 70             $ 430
1980      $ 62.2222        $ 367.778
1981      $ 54.4444        $ 313.333
1982      $ 46.6667        $ 266.667
1983      $ 38.8889        $ 227.778
1984      $ 31.111         $ 196.667
1985      $ 23.3333        $ 173.333
1986      $ 15.5555        $ 157.778
1987      $ 7.77778        $ 150
```

Program Listing

```
  5 CLS:P.:P.:P."SUM OF THE YEARS DIGITS DEPRECIATION":P.
 10 IN. "ENTER THE PRICE OF THE ASSET ";A:A=INT(A)
 20 IN. "ENTER THE SALVAGE VALUE OF THE ASSET";B:B=INT(B)
 30 IF A>B G. 40
 35 P. "SALVAGE MUST BE LESS THAN COST":G. 10
 40 C=A-B
 50 IN. "ENTER THE LIFE OF THE ASSET (YEARS)";D
 55 IN. "WHAT IS THE FIRST YEAR OF USE EX- 1979 ";G
 60 E=0:F=D
 70 E=E+D
 80 D=D-1
 90 IF D=0 G. 115
100 G. 70
115 CLS:P. "YEAR","DEPRECIATION","VALUE AT END OF YEAR"
130 H=C*(F/E)
140 A=A-H
145 P. G,"$";H,"$";A
150 F=F-1:G=G+1
160 IF F=0 G. 200
180 G. 130
200 END
```

Double Declining Balance Depreciation

This program calculates depreciation data connected with the Double Declining Balance method.

Variable List

C - Cost of asset.
S - Salvage value of asset.
L - Life of asset.
Y - Year of use.
B - Beginning book value for year Y.
T - Cumulative depreciation.
E - Ending book value for year Y.
D - Depreciation for year Y.

Suggested Variations

See second Suggested Variation for Straight Line Depreciation.

Sample Run

```
ENTER THE COST OF THE ASSET $?500
ENTER THE SALVAGE VALUE OF THE ASSET $?300
ENTER THE LIFE OF THE ASSET ?5
ENTER THE FIRST YEAR OF USE EX.--1979 ?1979
```

YEAR	COST	BOOK VAL	DEPREC	BOOK VAL	DEPREC
1979	500	500	200	300	200
1980	500	300	200	300	3.05E-05

Program Listing

```
 5 CLS:P.:P.:P."DOUBLE DECLINING BALANCE DEPRECIATION":P.
10 IN. "ENTER THE COST OF THE ASSET $";C
20 IN. "ENTER THE SALVAGE VALUE OF THE ASSET $";S
30 IF S>=C THEN P. "SALVAGE MUST BE LESS THAN COST":G. 10
40 IN. "ENTER THE LIFE OF THE ASSET";L
45 IN. "ENTER THE FIRST YEAR OF USE EX- 1979 ";Y
47 Y=Y-1:U=Y
50 T=0:E=0:B=C
60 R=((100/L)/100)*2
65 CLS
70 P.TAB(22);"BEGIN";TAB(33);"TOTAL";TAB(44);"END";TAB(55);"YEAR"
80 P."YEAR";TAB(11);"COST";TAB(22);"BOOK VAL";TAB(33);"DEPREC";
90 P.TAB(4)"BOOK VAL";TAB(55);"DEPREC"
```

```
100 P. "-------------------------------------"
110 Y=Y+1
120 D=B*R
130 E=B-D
140 T=T+D
150 IF E<=S G. 200
160 IF Y=(L+U) G. 270
170 GOS. 1000
180 B=E
190 G. 110
200 IF E=S G. 250
210 H=S-E
220 D=D-H
230 T=T-H
240 E=E+H
250 GOS. 1000
260 G. 320
270 H=E-S
280 D=D+H
290 T=T+H
300 E=E-H
310 GOS. 1000
320 END
1000 P.Y;TAB(11);C;TAB(22);B;TAB(33);T;TAB(44);E;TAB(55);D
1010 RETURN
```

Simple Inventory

This program will store and recall, as well as update, a 100 item or less stock.

Variable List

A - Menu choice.
B - Current item number.
N - Number of items.
S - Stock number of item B.
Q - Quantity of item B.
P - Price of item B.
A(B) - Code number of item B (corresponds to array location).
A(B+100) - Stock number of item B.
A(B+200) - Quantity of item B.
A(B+300) - Price of item B.
Z - Update or not.

Suggested Variations

■ Additional columns (retail price, on order, etc.) should be created as memory allows.

■ Stock maximum can be raised above 100 items by extending the separation of array locations for each column. If 150 items are needed, change A(B+100) to A(B+150), A(B+200) to A(B+250), etc.

Sample Run

```
THIS INVENTORY WILL HANDLE UP TO 100 ITEMS
DO YOU WANT TO:
1) ENTER A NEW INVENTORY LIST
2) UPDATE AN INVENTORY LIST
3) EXAMINE A SPECIFIC ITEM
ENTER YOUR CHOICE (l, 2, or 3)?2
PRINTING SEQUENCE
HAS TAPE FILE BEEN LOADED YET (1=YES 2=NO)?1
CODE        STOCK #        QUANT.        PRICE
1           25012          56            $ 2.59
2           3612           125           $ 2.3
3           65897          45            $ 7.95
4           25236          14            $ 13.99
   DO YOU WISH TO UPDATE AN ITEM (1=YES 2=NO)?2
```

Program Listing

```
  5 CLS:P.:P.:P."SIMPLE INVENTORY":P.
 10 P. "THIS INVENTORY WILL HANDLE UP TO 100 ITEMS."
 20 P. "DO YOU WANT TO:"
 30 P. "1) ENTER A NEW INVENTORY LIST"
 40 P. "2) UPDATE AN INVENTORY LIST"
 50 P. "3) EXAMINE A SPECIFIC ITEM"
 60 IN. "ENTER YOUR CHOICE (1, 2, OR 3) ";A
 70 IF A=1 G. 100
 80 IF A=2 G. 500
 90 IF A=3 G. 800
 95 G. 60
100 IN. "HOW MANY ITEMS";N
110 FOR B=1 TO N
115 P. "ITEM #";B
120 IN. "WHAT IS THE STOCK NUMBER";S
130 IN. "WHAT IS THE QUANTITY";Q
140 IN. "WHAT IS THE PRICE";P
150 A(B+100)=S:A(B+200)=Q:A(B+300)=P
160 N. B
170 P. "LISTING COMPLETE. TO SAVE ON TAPE, REWIND TAPE TO"
180 IN. "START. PRESS ENTER TO CONTINUE";A$:CLS
190 P. "DEPRESS BOTH RECORD AND PLAY KEYS ON RECORDER."
200 IN. "PRESS ENTER WHEN THIS IS DONE";A$:CLS
210 P. "LOADING ONTO TAPE: PLEASE WAIT."
220 FOR B=1 TO N
225 A(B)=B
230 PRINT # A(B);",";A(B+100);",";A(B+200);",";A(B+300)
240 N. B
250 CLS:G. 10
500 P. "PRINTING SEQUENCE"
```

```
505 IN. "HAS TAPE FILE BEEN LOADED YET (1=YES 2=NO)";W
507 IF W <> 1 G. 510
508 CLS: G. 540
510 P.:P. "TO UPDATE INVENTORY LIST, INSERT PROPER RECORD"
520 P. "TAPE INTO THE RECORDER AND DEPRESS THE PLAY KEY."
525 IN. "HOW MANY ITEMS ARE RECORDED ON THIS TAPE";E
530 IN. "PRESS ENTER TO LOAD TAPE FILE";A$:CLS
540 P. "CODE","STOCK #","QUANT.","PRICE"
545 FOR B=1 TO E
547 IF W=1 G. 560
550 INPUT # A(B),A(B+100),A(B+200),A(B+300)
560 P. A(B),A(B+100)A,(B+200),"$";A(B+300)
570 N. B
580 IN. "DO YOU WISH TO UPDATE AN ITEM (1=YES 2=NO)";Z
590 IF Z=1 G. 600
595 CLS:G. 10
600 IN. "WHAT IS THE PRODUCT'S CODE #";B
610 IN. "WHAT IS THE PRODUCT'S NEW STOCK #";A(B+100)
620 IN. "WHAT IS THE PRODUCT'S NEW QUANTITY";A(B+200)
630 IN. "WHAT IS THE PRODUCT'S NEW PRICE";A(B+300)
640 P. "UPDATE COMPLETE. TO STORE NEW DATA REWIND TAPE TO"
650 G. 180
800 P. "LISTING SEQUENCE"
810 IN. "HAS FILE TAPE BEEN LOADED YET? (1=YES 2=NO)";z
830 IF Z=1 G. 840
835 P. "PERFORM PRINTING SEQUENCE":G. 500
840 IN."WHAT IS THE PRODUCT'S CODE #";B
850 P. "CODE","STOCK #","QUANT.","PRICE"
855 P. A(B),A(B+100),A(B+200),A(B+300)
860 IN. "TO EXAMINE ANOTHER PRODUCT TYPE IN 1, OTHERWISE 2";Z
870 IF Z=1 G. 880
875 CLS:G. 10
880 G. 840
```

Mean, Standard Deviation, Standard Error of the Mean

This program calculates the mean, standard deviation, and standard error of the mean for a group of sample values. See Fig. 7-4.

Variable List

N - Number of samples.
C - Current sample number.
D - Value of sample C.
M - Mean.
S - Standard deviation.
G - Standard error of the mean.

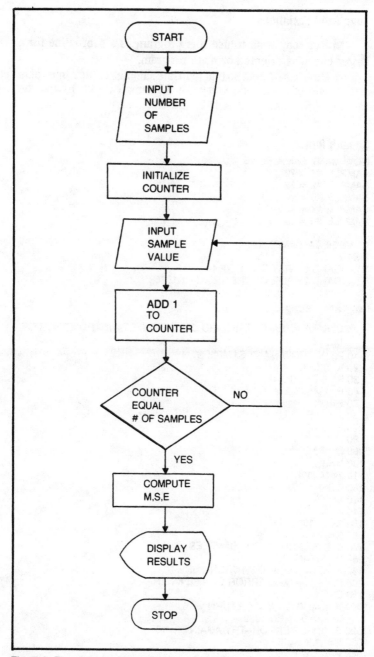

Fig. 7-4. Flowchart for Mean Standard Deviation, and Standard Error of the Mean program.

Suggested Variations

■ You may wish to use this program as a subroutine for a larger business oriented or math program.

■ Devise a system so that multiple samples of the same value can be entered with one entry.For 12 samples each having the value of 2.5, you can enter it 2.5,12.

Sample Run

```
HOW MANY SAMPLES ?5
SAMPLE #1 = ?2
SAMPLE #2 = ?9
SAMPLE #3 = ?6
SAMPLE #4 = ?5
SAMPLE #5 = ?4

NUMBER OF SAMPLES-- 5
MEAN-- 5.2
STANDARD DEVIATION-- 2.58844
STANDARD ERROR OF THE MEAN-- 1.15758
```

Program Listing

```
   5 CLS:P.:P."MEAN, STANDARD DEVIATION, STANDARD ERROR OF
     MEAN"
  10 P.: IN. "HOW MANY SAMPLES";N
  20 A=0:B=0
  30 FOR C=1 TO N
  40 P. "SAMPLE #";C;"=";:IN. D
  50 E=D*D
  60 A=A+E
  70 B=B+D
  80 N. C
  90 M=B/N
 100 D=B*B
 110 X=(A-D/N)/(N-1)
 120 GOS. 1000
 130 S=Y
 140 X=N
 150 GOS. 1000
 160 G=S/Y
 170 CLS:P. "NUMBER OF SAMPLES-- ";N
 180 P. "MEAN-- ";M
 190 P. "STANDARD DEVIATION-- ";S
 200 P. "STANDARD ERROR OF THE MEAN-- ";G
 210 END
1000 IF X=0 THEN Y=0:RETURN
1010 IF X > 0 THEN 1030
1020 P. "INPUT ERROR--TRY AGAIN";G. 10
1030 Y=X*.5:Z=0
1040 W=(X/Y-Y)*.5
1050 IF (W=0)+(W=Z) THEN RETURN
1060 Y=Y+W:Z=W:G. 1040
```

Economic Order Quantity

This program calculates the most economic quantity of units to order according to annual demand, price of each unit, and the cost of ordering and stocking each unit.

Variable List

C - Cost of each unit.
D - Demand of units annually.
H - Stocking costs.
S - Ordering costs.
Q - Economic order quantity.
T - Cost to order and stock an item at other values of Q.

Suggested Variations

■ This program will crash if Q=0. You may wish to devise a system that will print out a message like "Uneconomical to order at any quantity" when this occurs.

Sample Run

```
HOW MUCH DOES ONE UNIT COST $?1.25
HOW MANY UNITS DO YOU SELL PER YEAR ?250
HOW MUCH DOES IT COST TO STORE ONE UNIT FOR ONE YEAR $?.25
HOW MUCH DOES IT COST TO PLACE AN ORDER $?15.00
YOU SHOULD ORDER 173 UNITS PER ORDER
PRESS ENTER TO CONTINUE?
FOR ORDER QUANTITIES OF 114 UNITS, THE ANNUAL
COST TO ORDER AND STOCK THIS ITEM IS $ 47.1447
PRESS ENTER TO CONTINUE?
FOR ORDER QUANTITIES OF 171 UNITS, THE ANNUAL
COST TO ORDER AND STOCK THIS ITEM IS $ 43.3048
PRESS ENTER TO CONTINUE?
FOR ORDER QUANTITIES OF 228 UNITS, THE ANNUAL
COST TO ORDER AND STOCK THIS ITEM IS $ 44.9474
PRESS ENTER TO CONTINUE?
```

Program Listing

```
 5 CLS:P.:P.:P."ECONOMIC ORDER QUANTITY":P.
10 IN. "HOW MUCH DOES ONE UNIT COST $";C
20 IN. "HOW MANY UNITS DO YOU SELL PER YEAR ";D
30 IN. "HOW MUCH DOES IT COST TO STOCK ONE UNIT PER YEAR $";H
40 IN. "HOW MUCH DOES IT COST TO PLACE AN ORDER $";S
50 X=(2*D*S)/H
60 GOS. 1000
70 Q=INT(Y)
80 P. "YOU SHOULD ORDER ";Q;" UNITS PER ORDER."
```

```
 85 P.:P.:IN. "PRESS ENTER TO CONTINUE";A$:CLS
 90 Q=Q/3
100 Q=INT(Q)
110 R=Q
120 N=0
130 N=N+1
140 Q=Q+R
150 T=D/Q*S+Q/2*H
160 IF N > 7 G. 200
170 P. "FOR ORDER QUANTITIES OF ";Q;" UNITS, THE ANNUAL"
180 P. "COST TO ORDER AND STOCK THIS ITEM IS $";T
190 P.:P.:IN. "PRESS ENTER TO CONTINUE";A$:CLS:G. 130
200 IN."TYPE 1 TO CONTINUE OR 2 TO QUIT";G
210 IF G=1 G. 5
220 END
1000 IF X= 0 THEN Y=0:RET.
1010 IF X > 0 THEN 1020
1015 P. "YOU MADE AN INPUT MISTAKE. TRY AGAIN":G. 10
1020 Y=X*.5:Z=0
1030 W=(X*Y-Y)*.5
1040 IF (W=0)+(W=Z) THEN RETURN
1050 Y=Y+W:Z=W:G. 1030
```

Break Even Analysis

This program calculates the number of items that must be produced in order to break even after sales of all items has been completed.

Variable List

F - Fixed costs.
V - Direct cost of each unit produced.
P - Price of each unit as sold.
B - Break even quantity.
I - Total profit at production of B units.

Suggested Variations

■ You may wish to take this analysis one step farther by showing the total profit for production of units above B and below B.

Sample Run

ENTER THE FIXED COSTS THAT WOULD OCCUR NO MATTER
HOW MANY UNITS YOU PRODUCE $?150.00
ENTER THE DIRECT COST FOR EACH UNIT YOU PRODUCE $?1.52
HOW MUCH DO YOU SELL ONE UNIT FOR $?3.95
BREAK EVEN UNITS IS 62

AT THIS VOLUME (62 UNITS) TOTAL PROFIT =$ .66
TYPE 1 TO CONTINUE OR 2 TO QUIT?2

Program Listing

```
  5 CLS:P.:P.:P."BREAK EVEN ANALYSIS":P.
 10 P. "ENTER THE FIXED COSTS THAT WOULD OCCUR NO MATTER"
 20 IN. "HOW MANY UNITS YOU PRODUCE $";F
 30 IN. "ENTER THE DIRECT COST FOR EACH UNIT YOU PRODUCE $";V
 40 IN. "HOW MUCH DO YOU SELL ONE UNIT FOR $";P
 50 B=F/(P-V)
 60 B=INT(B)+1
 70 P. "BREAK EVEN UNITS IS ";B
 80 I=B*(P-V)-F
 82 I=I+.005:I=I*100:I=INT(I):I=I/100
 90 P. "AT THIS VOLUME (";B;"UNITS) TOTAL PROFIT = $";I
100 IN. "TYPE 1 TO CONTINUE OR 2 TO QUIT";T
110 IF T=1 G. 5
120 END
```

Chapter 8
Educational Programs

The programs in this chapter are meant to serve educational purposes. Please note that while none of these programs will teach a particular skill or vocation, they will increase the proficiency of a skill through repetition as well as interest and amusement.

The role of the computer in education has been a subject of controversy for some time now, and it is the intent of these programs to show that the computer can be used to aid the teacher, *not* replace him (Fig. 8-1).

Some of these programs are meant as a quiz in a particular subject area where the user interacts with the computer via the keyboard. Other programs are constructed to demonstrate a certain property or concept.

The educator, or concerned parent, should not overlook such programs as WORD QUIZ and both of the algebra quizzes. These can be easily modified to quiz on any subject area that can be expressed by multiple choice, true or false, or straight numeric answers.

Echo

The user must repeat a sequence of random numbers that are flashed on the screen briefly. This is a lot tougher than you might think, and you may even find your memory a lot sharper after a few rounds!

Fig. 8-1. The computer can be an aid to the teacher.

Variable List

G - Number of rounds.
X, Y - Timing loops.
A, B, C, D, E - Numbers 1-5 respectively.
I, J, K, L, M - User's guesses for numbers 1-5 respectively.
N - Number of numbers displayed in game (five numbers each round).

Suggested Variations

■ Change FOR-NEXT loops in Line #'s 90, 110, 130, 150, and 170 to vary amount of time each number is displayed.
■ Change number of numbers each round.
■ Devise a system to allow more than one player.

Sample Run

```
HOW MANY ROUNDS (FIVE NUMBERS EACH ROUND)?1
FIRST NUMBER:
8
SECOND NUMBER:
53
THIRD NUMBER
5
```

FOURTH NUMBER:
66
FIFTH NUMBER:
50
###########################
WHAT WAS THE FIRST NUMBER?8
CORRECT
WHAT WAS THE SECOND NUMBER?53
CORRECT!
WHAT WAS THE THIRD NUMBER?15
WHAT WAS THE FOURTH NUMBER?66
CORRECT!
WHAT WAS THE FIFTH NUMBER?50
CORRECT!
------------ FINAL RESULTS ------------------
OUT OF 5 NUMBERS, YOU GUESSED 4 CORRECTLY

Program Listing

```
  5 CLS:P.:P.:P."ECHO":P.
 10 P. "FIVE RANDOM NUMBERS WILL FLASH ON THE SCREEN FOR":Z=0
 20 P. "APPROX. ½ SECOND. YOU MUST THEN PUT THEM IN"
 30 P. "CORRECT SEQUENCE IN ORDER TO RECEIVE POINTS."
 40 IN. "HOW MANY ROUNDS (FIVE NUMBERS EACH ROUND)";G
 50 FOR H=1 TO G
 60 CLS:P. "ROUND #";H
 70 IN. "PRESS ENTER TO START ROUND";A$:CLS
 80 P. "FIRST NUMBER:":FOR X=1 TO 500:N.X
 90 A=RND(100):P. A:FOR Y=1 TO 250:N. Y
100 CLS:P. "SECOND NUMBER:":FOR X=1 TO 500:N.X.
110 B=RND(100):P. B:FOR Y=1 TO 250:N. Y
120 CLS:P. "THIRD NUMBER:":FOR X=1 TO 500 :N.X
130 C=RND(100):P. C:FOR Y=1 TO 250:N. Y
140 CLS:P. "FOURTH NUMBER:":FOR X=1 TO 500:N.X
150 D=RND(⅛00):P.D:FOR Y=1 TO 250:N.Y
160 CLS:P. "FIFTH NUMBER:":FOR X=1 TO 500:N.X
170 E=RND(100):P.E.:FOR Y=1 TO 250:N. Y
180 CLS
190 P. "********************"
200 IN. "WHAT WAS THE FIRST NUMBER";I
202 IF I=A THEN Z=Z+1:P. "CORRECT!"
210 IN. "WHAT WAS THE SECOND NUMBER";J
212 IF J=B THEN Z=Z+1:P. "CORRECT!"
220 IN. "WHAT WAS THE THIRD NUMBER";K
222 IF K=C THEN Z=Z+1:P. "CORRECT!"
230 IN. "WHAT WAS THE FOURTH NUMBER";L
232 IF L=D THEN Z=Z+1:P. "CORRECT!"
240 IN. "WHAT WAS THE FIFTH NUMBER";M
242 IF M=E THEN Z=Z+1:P. "CORRECT!"
245 FOR V=1 TO 1500:N.V: CLS
250 N.H
260 P. "------------- FINAL RESULTS ----------------"
265 N=G*5
270 P. "OUT OF";N;"NUMBERS, YOU GUESSED";Z;"CORRECTLY."
280 END
```

156

Math Teacher

This program improves the mathematics aptitude. It is especially good for kids who aren't excited even by calculators.

Variable List

A - Number of questions.
C - Correct responses.
I - Incorrect responses.
B - Problem type choice.
N - Question number.
E, F - Numbers used in equations.
G - Player's answer to equation.
H - Actual answer to equation.
T - Percent of total questions answered correctly.

Suggested Variations

■ Change range of numbers in the equations.
■ Add more choices of equation types.
■ Note the system used to insure a whole number answer for division problems (Line #320). You may wish to remove this for a more advanced student.

Sample Run

```
HOW MANY QUESTIONS?2
ENTER 1 FOR ADDITION, 2 FOR SUBTRACTION, 3 FOR
DIVISION, OR 4 FOR MULTIPLICATION?4
SCRATCH PAPER NOT ALLOWED!
QUESTION # 1
12 × 5 = ?60
ABSOLUTELY CORRECT!
QUESTION # 2
9 × 3 = ?27
ABSOLUTELY CORRECT!
FINAL    TALLY
--------------------
CORRECT ANSWERS---- 2
INCORRECT ANSWERS-- 0
100 % FOR THIS EXERCISE
```

Program Listing

```
  5 CLS:P.:P.:P."MATH TEACHER":P.
 10 IN."HOW MANY QUESTIONS";A
 20 C=0:I=0
 30 P. "ENTER 1 FOR ADDITION, 2 FOR SUBTRACTION, 3 FOR"
 50 IN. "DIVISION, OR 4 FOR MULTIPLICATION";B
 60 P. "SCRATCH PAPER NOT ALLOWED!":FOR Z=
 70 IF B=1 G. 100
 71 IF B=2 G. 200
 72 IF B = 3 G. 300
 73 IF B=4 G. 400
 75 P."ILLEGAL PROBLEM CHOICE—FOLLOW DIRECTIONS!":G.30
100 FOR N=1 TO A
110 P. "QUESTION #";N
120 E=RND(1000):F=RND(1000)
130 P.E;" + ";F;" = ";
140 IN. G:H=E+F
150 IF G=H G. 160
152 P. "NOPE, THAT'S NOT CORRECT."
157 I=I+1: G. 175
160 P. "ABSOLUTELY CORRECT!"
165 C=C+1
175 N.N
180 G. 500
200 FOR N=1 TO A
210 P."QUESTION #";N
220 E=RND(1000):=RND(1000)
230 P.E;"-";F;" = ";
240 IN. G:H=E-F
250 IF G=H G. 160
260 G. 152
300 FOR N=1 TO A
310 P. "QUESTION #";N
320 E=RND 10):F=RND(1000)*E
330 P.F;"/";E;" = ";
340 IN. G:H=F/E
350 IF G=H G. 160
360 G. 152
400 FOR N=1 TO A
410 P."QUESTION #";N
420 E=RND(15):F=RND(15)
430 P.E;"X";F;"=";
440 IN.G:H=E*F
450 IF G=H G. 160
455 G.152
500 FOR Z=1 TO 1000:N.Z:CLS
510 P."FINAL TALLY"
515 P."------------"
520 P. "CORRECT ANSWERS---";C
525 P. "INCORRECT ANSWERS--";I
530 P.
540 T=C/A*100:T.T;"% FOR THIS EXERCISE"
550 END
```

Algebra Quiz I

This program teaches the Distributive Axiom of Multiplication with Respect to Addition (Fig. 8-2). It can be a challenging and fun quiz for students of all ages. Just remember that for all real numbers A, B, and C:

$$A(B+C)=A(B)+A(C)$$

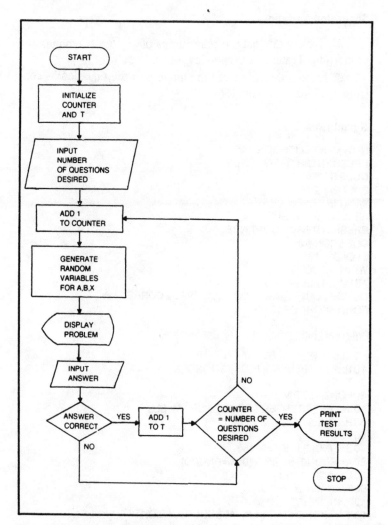

Fig. 8-2. Flowchart for algebra quiz I

Variable List

N - Number of questions.

Z - Question number.

E - Decides problem type.

A, B, X - Numbers used in problem.

V - Player's solution of X.

X - Answer to equation.

T - Number of correct answers.

Suggested Variations

■ Expand this quiz to other areas of algebra (Commutative properties, Transitive properties, etc.).

■ Extend the range of the numbers in the equation as controlled in Line #'s 80 and 150.

Sample Run

```
HOW MANY QUESTIONS?2
PRESS ENTER TO CONTINUE?
QUESTION # 1
3 (X − 2) = 24
WHAT IS X? 10
ABSOLUTELY RIGHT!
PRESS ENTER TO CONTINUE?
QUESTION # 2
8 (X + 3) = 64
WHAT IS X?5
ABSOLUTELY RIGHT!
OUT OF 2 QUESTIONS, YOU ANSWERED 2 CORRECTLY
FOR A SCORE OF 100 %
```

Program Listing

```
  5 CLS:P.:P.:P. "ALGEBRA QUIZ I":P.
 10 P.:P.:IN. "HOW MANY QUESTIONS";N
 20 T=0
 30 FOR Z=1 TO N
 40 IN. "PRESS ENTER TO CONTINUE";A$:CLS
 50 P. "QUESTION #";Z
 60 P.
 70 E=RND(2):IF E=1 G. 150
 80 A=RND(10):B=RND(10):X=RND(10)
 90 C=(A*X)+(A*B)
100 P. A;"(X+";B;")=";C
110 P.:IN. "WHAT IS X";V
120 IF V=X THEN T=T+1:P. "ABSOULTELY RIGHT!"
130 IF V<>X THEN P. "WRONG. X=";X
```

```
140 G. 200
150 A=RND(10):B=RND(10):X=RND(10):IF X<B G. 150
160 C=(A*X)-(A*B)
170 P. A;"(X - ";B;")=";C
180 G. 110
200 N. Z
210 P.:P
215 P. "FINAL SCORE"
220 P. "OUT OF ";Z- 1; "QUESTIONS, YOU ANSWERED ";T; "CORRECT-
    LY."
230 P. "FOR A SCORE OF ";T/(Z- 1)*100; "%"
230 END
```

Algebra Quiz II

This program challenges the user to extract the binomial roots of simple polynomials. Example:

$X^2 + 4X - 60$ roots are $(X + 10)$ and $(X - 6)$.

Variable List

N - Number of questions.

Z - Question number.

T - Number of correct answers.

E - Decides if A and B are positive or negative.

A, B - Actual roots of polynomial.

C, D - Numbers used in polynomial equation.

G, H - Player's solution of A and B

Suggested Variations

■ Extend the range of the polynomial as controlled in Line #'s 50 and 60.

■ You may wish, if you have the memory, to combine this program with Algebra Quiz I.

Sample Run

```
HOW MANY QUESTIONS?2
PRESS ENTER TO CONTINUE?
QUESTION # 1
EQUATION--
X SQUARED - 15 X + 56
WHAT ARE THE ROOTS?
X?-7
AND... X?-8
```

RIGHT!
PRESS ENTER TO CONTINUE?
QUESTION # 2
EQUATION--
X SQUARE – 1 × –56
WHAT ARE THE ROOTS?
X? –8
AND... X?+7
RIGHT!
OUT OF 2 QUESTIONS YOU ANSWERED 2 CORRECTLY
FOR A SCORE OF 100%

Program Listing

```
  5 CLS:P.:P.:P."ALGEBRA QUIZ II":P.
 10 P.:P.:IN. "HOW MANY QUESTIONS ";N
 15 T=0
 20 FOR Z=1 TO N
 30 IN. "PRESS ENTER TO CONTINUE";A$:CLS
 40 P."QUESTION #";Z
 50 A=RND(10):E=RND(2):IF E=2 THEN A=–A
 60 B=RND(10):E=RND(2):IF E=2 THEN B=–B
 70 C=A+B:D=A*B
 80 P."EQUATION--";P.:P."X SQUARED ";:IF C 0 THEN P. "+";
 90 P.C;"X";:IF D 0 THEN P."+";
100 P.D
110 P.:P
120 P."WHAT ARE THE ROOTS?"
130 IN."X";G
135 IF (G=A)+(G=B) G. 200
140 P."WRONG. THE ROOTS WERE X";:IF A>0 THEN P. "+";
150 P.A;"      AND      X";:IF B>0 THEN P. "+";
160 P.B
170 N.Z
180 P."OUT OF ";Z–1; " QUESTIONS YOU ANSWERED ";T;
"CORRECTLY."
190 P."FOR A SCORE OF ";T/(Z–1)*100;"%"
195 END
200 IF G=A G. 250
210 IN. "AND... X";H
220 IF H=A G. 230
225 G. 140
230 P."RIGHT!":T=T+1:G. 170
250 IN."AND... X";H
260 IF H=B G. 230
270 G. 140
```

Word Quiz

This program tests the player's ability to identify spelling
errors. A list of five words is displayed on the screen, the player
must then identify the one that is misspelled.

Variable List

R - Number of correct answers.
A - Player's guess of misspelled word.
(that's all!)

Suggested Variations

■ This program may be extended for as many questions as your memory will handle.

■ You may wish to devise a system to print lists of words read randomly from a DATA statement(s) in the program.

Sample Run

```
QUESTION # 1
WHICH OF THESE WORDS ARE MISSPELLED:
1)DUNGEON   2) DISSENTION   3) DISPUTANT   4)DIADEM
?4
WRONG. NUMBER 2 WAS MISSPELLED.
PRESS ENTER TO CONTINUE?
QUESTION # 2
WHICH OF THESE WORDS ARE MISSPELLED:
1) BALANCER 2) BALKEY 3) BANZAI 4) BARLEY
?2
RIGHT! CORRECT SPELLING: BALKY
PRESS ENTER TO CONTINUE?
```

Program Listing

```
  5 CLS:P.:P.:P. "WORD QUIZ":P
 10 R=0
 20 GOS. 1000
 30 P. "QUESTION #1"
 40 P.:P.
 50 P. "WHICH OF THESE WORDS ARE MISSPELLED:"
 60 P. "1) DUNGEON 2)DISSENTION 3) DISPUTANT 4) DIADEM"
 70 IN. A
 80 IF A=2 THEN P."RIGHT! CORRECT SPELLING: DISSENSION":R=R+1
 90 IF A <> 2 THEN P. "WRONG. NUMBER 2 WAS MISSPELLED."
100 GOS. 1000
110 P. "QUESTION #2"
120 P.:P.
130 P. "WHICH OF THESE WORDS ARE MISSPELLED:"
140 P. "1)BALANCER 2)BALKEY 3)BANZAI 4)BARLEY"
150 IN. A
160 IF A=2 THEN P. "RIGHT! CORRECT SPELLING: BALKY":R=R+1
170 IF A <> 2 THEN P. "WRONG. NUMBER 2 WAS MISSPELLED."
180 GOS. 1000
190 P. "QUESTION#3"
200 P.:P.
210 P. "WHICH OF THESE WORDS ARE MISSPELLED:"
```

```
220 P. "1) FRINGY 2) FRONTIER 3) FRONTAGE 4)FRUGALY"
230 IN. A
240 IF A=4 THEN P. "RIGHT! CORRECT SPELLING: FRUGALLY":R=R+1
250 IF A <>4 THEN P. "WRONG. NUMBER 4 WAS MISSPELLED."
260 GOS. 1000
270 P. "QUESTION #4"
275 P.:P.
280 P. "WHICH OF THESE WORDS ARE MISSPELLED:"
290 P. "1) JUGULAR 2) JINGOISTIC 3) JAUNTILEY 4) JAGUAR"
300 IN. A
310 IF A=3 THEN P. "RIGHT! CORRECT SPELLING: JAUNTILY":R=R+1
320 IF A <> 3 THEN P. "WRONG. NUMBER 3 WAS MISSPELLED."
330 GOS. 1000
340 P. "QUESTION #5"
350 P.:P.
360 P. "WHICH OF THESE WORDS ARE MISSPELLED."
370 P. "1) SONOROUS 2) SKETCHEY 3) SIREN 4) SINISTER"
380 IN. A
390 IF A=2 THEN  P. "RIGHT! CORRECT    SPELLING:
    SKETCHY":R=R+1
400 IF A <> 2 THEN P. "WRONG. NUMBER 2 WAS MISPELLED."
410 GOS. 1000
420 P. "YOUR SCORE FOR THIS TEST IS";R/5*100;"%"
430 END
1000 IN. "PRESS ENTER TO CONTINUE"; A$:CLS
1010 RETURN
```

Calculated Dice Throws

This program will throw 1, 2, or 3 dice a specified number of
times and then print out a table showing the results of each throw
possibility.

Variable List

A(I) - Number of times the total spots I has been thrown.

A - Number of dice.

N - Number of throws.

X - Throw number.

D, E, F - Die 1, Die 2, Die 3.

J - Die 1 on single die throws, also total spots thrown each throw.

Suggested Variations

▓ Allow more than 3 dice to be thrown.

▓ Print a table showing the desired percentages for a true
random number generation.

164

Sample Run

```
HOW MANY DICE (1, 2, OR 3)?2
HOW MANY THROWS?1000
```

TOTAL	OCCURANCE	PERCENT
2	25	2.5
3	54	5.4
4	76	7.6
5	112	11.2
6	134	13.4
7	183	18.3
8	139	13.9
9	98	9.8
10	87	8.7
11	58	5.8
12	34	3.4

Program Listing

```
  5 CLS:P.:P.:P."CALCULATED DICE THROWS":P.
 10 FOR I=1 TO 18:A(I)=0:N. I
 20 IN. "HOW MANY DICE (1, 2, OR 3) ";A
 30 IN. "HOW MANY THROWS";N
 40 FOR X=1 TO: N
 50 CLS:P. "CALCULATING THROW #";X
 60 IF A=1 THEN 100
 70 IF A=2 THEN 120
 80 IF A=3 THEN 140
 90 P. "ILLEGAL NUMBER OF DICE":STOP
100 J=RND(6)
110 G. 200
120 D=RND(6):E=RND(6):J=D+E
130 G. 200
140 D=RND(6):E=RND(6):F=RND(6):J=D+E+F
200 A(J)=A(J)+1
210 N. X
220 CLS
230 P. "TOTAL    OCCURRANCE    PERCENT"
240 FOR J=1 TO 6
242 IF A=2 THEN 300
245 IF A=3 THEN 350
250 P. J;"    ";A(J);"    ";A(J)/N*100
260 N. J
270 G. 400
300 FOR J=2 TO 12
310 P. J;"    ";A(J);"    ";A(J)/N*100
320 N. J
330 G. 400
350 FOR J=3 TO 10
360 P. J;"    ";A(J);"    ";A(J)/N*100
370 N. J
380 IN. "PRESS ENTER TO COMPLETE LIST";A$:CLS
381 P. "TOTAL    OCCURRANCE    PERCENT"
382 FOR J=11 TO 18
390 P. J;"    ";A(J);"    ";A(J);"    ";A(J)/N*100
395 N. J
400 END
```

165

Acceleration of a Falling Body in a Vacuum

This program calculates the acceleration due to gravity and the current altitude for each second until impact for a body falling in a vacuum (Fig. 8-3).

Variable List

A - Altitude.
D - Seconds.
C - Acceleration of falling body.
T - Print out control.
G - Continue or quit.

Suggested Variations

■ Allow user to check progress of falling body at intervals other than 1 second.
■ Allow the user to enter the desired initial velocity.

Sample Run

```
WHAT IS THE INITIAL ALTITUDE (FEET) ?1000
SECONDS     ALTITUDE (FT)    VELOCITY (FT/SEC)
   0           1000               0
   1          967.826           32.174
   2          903.478           64.348
   3          806.956           96.522
   4          678.26           128.696
   5          517.39           160.87
   6          324.346          193.044
   7           99.1283         225.218
   8          IMPACT           257.392
TYPE 1 TO CONTINUE OR 0 TO QUIT?0
```

Program Listing

```
 5 CLS:p.:P.:P."ACCELERATION OF A FALLING BODY IN A VACUUM":P.
10 IN. "WHAT IS THE INITIAL ALTITUDE (FEET) ";A
30 D=0:C=0
35 T=0:CLS
40 P. "SECONDS","ALTITUDE (FT)","VELOCITY (FT/SEC)"
50 P. D,A,C
60 D=D+1
```

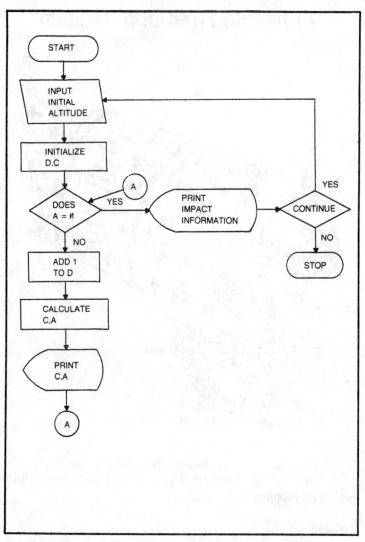

Fig. 8-3. Flowchart for acceleration of a falling body in a vacuum.

```
 70 C=C+32.174
 80 A=A-C:IF A< =0 G. 120
 85 T=T+1:IF T=13 G. 100
 90 G. 50
100 IN. "PRESS ENTER TO CONTINUE";A$
110 G. 35
120 P. D,"IMPACT",C
140 IN. "TYPE 1 TO CONTINUE OR 2 TO QUIT";G
145 IF G=1 G. 5
150 END
```

Projectile Fired in a Vacuum

This program calculates data pertaining to the flight of a projectile launched in a vacuum at a velocity and angle to the horizontal supplied by the user.

Variable List

V - Velocity.
A - Angle to the horizontal.
D - Total time of flight.
C - Time to highest altitude.
E - Maximum altitude.
G - Total horizontal range (displacement).
H - Continue or quit.
X, Y, Z - Used in sine subroutine.

Suggested Variations

■ This is an excellent program to dress up with some graphics.

■ Add an air resistance (friction) factor, or allow the user to supply one.

Sample Run

```
WHAT VELOCITY (FT/SEC) IS THE PROJECTILE FIRED AT ?550
AT WHAT ANGLE TO THE HORIZONTAL ?45
PROJECTILE FIRED IN A VACUUM AT 550 FEET/SEC
   45 DEGREES TO THE HORIZONTAL:

-----------------------------------------------------------------------------------
TOTAL TIME OF FLIGHT-------------------- 24.1753 SECONDS
TIME TO HIGHEST ALTITUDE------------- 12.0877 SECONDS
 MAXIMUM ATITUDE----------------------------2350.5 FEET
TOTAL HORIZONTAL RANGE--------------9402.03 FEET

TYPE 1 TO CONTINUE OR 2 TO QUIT?2
```

Program Listing

```
   5 CLS:P.:P.:P."PROJECTILE FIRED IN A VACUUM":P.
  10 IN. "WHAT VELOCITY (FT/SEC) IS PROJECTILE FIRED AT ";V
  20 IN. "AT WHAT ANGLE TO THE HORIZONTAL ";A
  30 X=A
  40 GOS. 1000
  50 C=(V*Y)/32.174
  60 D=((2*V*Y)/32.174
  70 E=((V*V)*(Y*Y))/64.348
  80 X=2*A
  90 GOS. 1000
 100 G=((V*V)*Y)/32.174
 110 CLS
 120 P. "PROJECTILE FIRED IN A VACUUM AT ";V;" FEET-SEC."
 130 P. A;" DEGREES TO THE HORIZONTAL:"
 140 P. "-----------------------------------------------------------------------------------
 150 P. "TOTAL TIME OF FLIGHT---------------- ";D;" SECONDS"
 160 P. "TIME TO HIGHEST ALTITUDE----------- ";C;" SECONDS"
 170 P. "MAXIMUM ALTITUDE-------------------- ";E;" FEET"
 180 P. "TOTAL HORIZONTAL RANGE------------- ";G;" FEET"
 190 P.:P.:IN. "TYPE 1 TO CONTINUE OR 2 TO QUIT ";H
 200 IF H= 1 G. 5
 210 END
1000 Z=ABS(X)/X:X=Z*X
1010 IF X>360 THEN X=X/360:X=(X- INT(X))*360
1020 IF X>90 THEN X=X/90:Y=INT(X):X=(X- Y)*90:ON Y G.
     1050,1060,1070
1030 X=X/57.29578:IF ABS(X) 2.48616E-4 THEN Y=0:RETURN
1040 G. 1080
1050 X=90-X:G. 1030
1060 X=-X:G. 1030
1070 X=X-90:G. 1030
1080 Y=X- X*X*X/6+X*X*X*X*X/120- X*X*X*X*X*X*X/5040
```

169

```
1090 Y=Y+X*X*X*X*X*X*X*X*X/362880:IF Z=-1 THEN Y=-Y
1100 RETURN
```

Permutations And Combinations

This program calculates the permutations and combinations according to the specified number of items and specified size of groups. See Fig. 8-4.

Variable List

B, A, C, T - Used in factorial subroutine: B is A!.
D - Number of items available.
E - Size of the groups under consideration.
P - Permutations.
C - Combinations.

Suggested Variations

■ Line #s 18 through 45 are a factorial subroutine. You may wish to extract this as a stand-alone program or for use in other larger programs.

Sample Run

```
HOW MANY ITEMS AVAILABLE?9
WHAT IS THE SIZE OF THE GROUPS UNDER CONSIDERATION?2
PERMUTATIONS-----  72
COMBINATIONS-----  36
```

Program Listing

```
  5 CLS:P.:P.:P. "PERMUTATIONS AND COMBINATIONS":P.
 10 G. 50
 15 REM***FACTORIAL SUBROUTINE IN A/OUT B USES C,T INTERNALLY
 18 B=A
 20 C=A-1
 25 FOR T=C TO 1 STEP -1
 30 B=B*T
 40 N. T
 45 RETURN
 50 IN. "HOW MANY ITEMS AVAILABLE";D
 60 IN. "WHAT IS THE SIZE OF THE GROUPS UNDR CONSIDERATION";E
 70 A=D
 80 GOS. 18
 90 F=B
100 A=D-E
110 GOS. 18
120 G=B
130 A=E
```

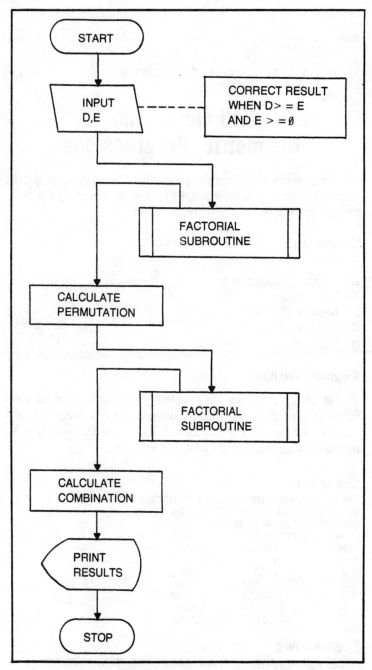

Fig. 8-4. Flowchart for the permutations and combinations program.

```
140 GOS. 18
150 H=B
160 P=F/G:C=F/(H*G)
170 P. 'PERMUTATIONS----- ";P
180 P. "COMBINATIONS----- ";C
190 IN. "TYPE 1 TO CONTINUE OR 2 TO QUIT";Z
200 IF Z=1 G. 5
210 END
```

Arithmetic and Geometric Progressions

This program will compute a specified number of terms with a common difference or ratio and the first term defined by the user for a geometric or arithmetic progression.

Variable List

D - Common difference or ratio.
E - Term value.
F - Number of terms.
C - Term number.
B - Sum.

Suggested Variation

■ To make this a more complete progression program, you might wish to include a process to compute harmonic progressions. For the numbers A and B with a difference of D, term N in a harmonic progression will equal $A/B+(N-1)D$.

Sample Run

```
TYPE 1 FOR ARITHMETIC OR 2 FOR GEOMETRIC ?2
WHAT IS THE RATIO OF TERMS ?7.25
WHAT IS THE FIRST TERM ?5
HOW MANY TERMS ?6
```

TERM #	VALUE	SUM
1	5	5
2	36.25	41.25
3	262.812	304.062
4	1905.39	2209.45
5	13814.1	16023.5
6	100152	116176

Program Listing

```
 5 CLS:P.:P.:P."ARITHMETIC AND GEOMETRIC PROGRESSIONS":P.
10 IN. "TYPE 1 FOR ARITHMETIC OR 2 FOR GEOMETRIC";A
```

```
 20 IF A=2 G. 500
 30 IF A <> 1 G. 10
 40 IN. "WHAT IS THE COMMON DIFFERENCE";D
 50 IN. "WHAT IS THE FIRST TERM";E
 60 IN. "HOW MANY TERMS";F
 62 CLS
 65 B=0
 80 C=1                    •
 83 P. "TERM #","VALUE","SUM"
 85 B=B+E
100 P. C,E,B
110 C=C+1:IF C>F G. 200
120 E=E+D
130 G. 85
200 END
500 IN. "WHAT IS THE RATIO OF TERMS";D
510 IN. "WHAT IS THE FIRST TERM";E
520 IN. "HOW MANY TERMS";F
522 CLS
525 B=0
530 C=1
533 P. "TERM #", "VALUE", "SUM"
535 B=B+E
540 P. C,E,B
550 C=C+1: IF C> F G. 200
560 E=E*D
570 G. 535
```

Base To Decimal Converter

Here's a handy program to convert any base (from Base 2 to Base 9) number up to ten digits in length to the decimal (Base 10) equivalent.

Variable List

B - Base.

A(V) - Calculated value of each digits place from 1 to 10.

D - Length of base number.

H - Digit number.

E - Value of Digit H.

G - Base 10 equivalent of base number.

Suggested Variations

■ Devise a system to convert one base number to another base other than 10.

■ Allow conversions of higher bases than Base 9.

Sample Run

WHAT BASE (2 TO 9) ?5
THE BASE NUMBER MAY BE UP TO 10 DIGITS LONG.

HOW MANY DIGITS LONG IS BASE NUMBER ?4
ENTER DIGITS AS READ FROM LEFT TO RIGHT.
DIGIT # 1 -- WHAT IS THE VALUE ?3
DIGIT # 2 -- WHAT IS THE VALUE ?0
DIGIT # 3 -- WHAT IS THE VALUE ?4
DIGIT # 4 -- WHAT IS THE VALUE ?2
3 0 4 2 BASE 5 EQUALS 397 BASE 10.

Program Listing

```
5 CLS:P.:P.:P."BASE TO DECIMAL CONVERSION":P.
10 IN. "WHAT BASE (2 TO 9) ";B
15 IF (B<2)+(B>9) THEN P. "INVALID BASE":G. 10
20 C=1
25 A(1)=1
30 FOR V=2 TO 10
40 C=C*B
50 A(V)=C
60 N. V
100 CLS:P. "THE BASE NUMBER MAY BE UP TO 10 DIGITS LONG."
110 IN. "HOW MANY DIGITS LONG IS BASE NUMBER ";D
112 IF (D>10)+(D<1) THEN P. "DIGIT IS TOO LONG":G. 100
115 P. "ENTER DIGITS AS READ FROM LEFT TO RIGHT."
120 G=0
125 F=99
130 FOR H=1 TO D
140 P. "DIGIT #";H;"-- WHAT IS THE VALUE ";:IN. E
150 IF E>=B THEN P. "INVALID BASE NOTATION":G. 140
155 K=(D-H)+1
160 G=G+(E*A(K))
163 F=F+1
165 A(F)=E
170 N. H
200 L=(D-1)+100
205 FOR I=100 TO L
210 P. A(I);
220 N. I
230 P. " BASE ";B;" EQUALS ";G;" BASE 10."
240 END
```

Detective's Dilemma

This program nearly ended up in the Games chapter, but instead landed here because of the fact that with a little imagination and revamping this can be a fine program to teach deductive reasoning.

Variable List

C - Number of bullets left in gun.
A - Guilty man.

B - Man who jumps out.

A$ - Man #B's name.

Q - Shoot or not.

V - Identification of guilty man when ammo is depleted.

T - Status to show if above is being executed (I. D. of guilty man).

Suggested Variations

■ Change number of suspects and killers.

■ Change number of bullets as controlled in Line #10

■ Devise a status system so that if an innocent bum is shot, he will not reappear again.

■ Add a system so that if an innocent man is shot, the killer is changed.

Sample Run

```
FILTHY FRANK JUMPS OUT OF THE DARKNESS AND CONFRONTS YOU!
DO YOU WISH TO SHOOT AT HIM(1=YES 2=NO)?2
FILTHY FRANK SLINKS BACK INTO THE DARKNESS
YOU HAVE 2 BULLET(S) REMAINING IN YOUR GUN
BUGSY MCCOY JUMPS OUT OF THE DARKNESS AND CONFRONTS YOU!
DO YOU WISH TO SHOOT AT HIM(1=YES 2=NO)?1
YES! BUGSY MCCOY WAS INDEED THE KILLER!
BUT HOW DID YOU FIGURE IT OUT, SHERLOCK?
```

Program Listing

```
  5 CLS:p.:P.:P."DETECTIVE'S DILEMMA":P.
 10 P.:C=2:A=RND(5):E=0:T=0
 20 P. "IN A DARK BUILDING WITH ONLY 2 BULLETS"
 30 P. "REMAINING IN YOUR GUN, YOU ARE HOT ON THE"
 40 P. "TRAIL OF A DANGEROUS KILLER. THERE ARE 5"
 50 P. "MEN IN THE BUILDING, BUT ONLY 1 IS THE"
 60 P. "KILLER. THE OTHER 4 ARE INNOCENT BUMS."
 70 P.:IN. "PRESS ENTER TO START THE GAME ";A$:CLS
 90 P. "YOU HAVE ";C; " BULLETS REMAINING IN YOUR GUN."
110 B=RND(5)
120 IF B=1 THEN A$=FILTHY FRANK
130 IF B=2 THEN A$=MUDDY MIKE
140 IF B=3 THEN A$=HORRIBLE HANK
150 IF B=4 THEN A$=BUGSY MCCOY
160 IF B=5 THEN A$=DIRTY DAN
165 IF T=1 G. 390
170 P.:P.:P.:P. A$;" JUMPS OUT OF THE DARKNESS AND CONFRONTS
    YOU!"
180 IN. "DO YOU WISH TO SHOOT AT HIM (1=YES 2=NO)";Q
190 IF Q=2 G. 250
200 C=C-1
210 IF B=A G. 220
215 P. "OH NO! YOU'VE KILLED AN INNOCENT BUM!"
217 IF C=0 G. 300
```

```
218 G. 90
220 P. "YES! ";A$;" WAS INDEED THE KILLER!"
230 P. "BUT HOW DID YOU FIGURE IT OUT, SHERLOCK?"
240 END
250 IF B=A G. 280
260 P. A$;" SLINKS BACK INTO THE DARKNESS-- HE'S A BUM!"
270 G. 90
280 P. A$;" DRAWS HIS GUN AND FIRES AT YOU!"
290 P. "SORRY, BUT HE BLEW YOUR BRAINS OUT."
295 G. 240
300 P. "AND YOU'RE OUT OF AMMO. HOWEVER, SINCE I'M A SPORTING"
310 P. "GUY, I'LL GIVE YOU ONE MORE CHANCE, IF YOU CAN IDENTIFY"
320 P. "THE KILLER, HE WILL SURRENDER. IF NOT, YOU WILL FIND"
330 P. "OUT THE HARD WAY WHO THE REAL KILLER IS."
340 P. "ENTER 1 FOR FILTHY FRANK, 2 FOR MUDDY MIKE"
350 P. "3 FOR HORRIBLE HANK, 4 FOR BUGSY MCCOY,"
360 IN. "OR 5 FOR DIRTY DAN";V
370 CLS: IF V=A G. 400
380 B=A:T=1 G. 120
390 G. 280
400 P. "YES!! IT'S ME! I GIVE UP! DON'T SHOOT ME, I GIVE UP!"
410 END
```

Glossary

The following is a list of words, terminology, and jargon which should help you in your further studies of the BASIC language.

algorithm - a precise set of rules which dictate a solution to a particular problem.

alphanumeric - any letter, number, or special symbol (including punctuation marks) which are used to convey a message.

AND - a logical operator used in conjunction with other logical operators to evaluate an arithmetic expression. In the statement: IF (A=1) AND (B=1) THEN Q=Q+1; Q will equal Q+1 only if A=1 *and* B=1.

ANSI - American National Standards Institute, which is responsible for many industry standards.

array - a series of ordered variables arranged in a list.

ASCII - American Standard Code for Information Interchange, responsible for many of the standards which allow compatibility between different brands and styles of computers.

BASIC - Beginner's All-purpose Symbolic Instruction Code, developed at Dartmouth College in order to simplify the use of computers.

baud - a measure of the speed of transmission of data. One baud equals one bit per second.

bit - a single character (usually represented as a 1 or a 0) which is the smallest unit of information a computer can utilize.

branch - a deviation from the chronological sequence of instructions performed by the computer.

byte - a number of bits (usually eight) which corresponds to a alpha-numeric character.

compiler - a built-in program which translates a high level computer language (such as BASIC) into machine language.

CPU - Central Processing Unit, the heart of the computer which interprets and executes machine language instructions.

CRT - Cathode Ray Tube. A video screen used for instantaneous communication between the user and the computer.

data - any information processed by the computer.

debug - to locate and correct errors (referred to as "bugs") in a program.

decimal - the numbers used in the base 10 system of numeric expression.

flowchart - a diagram to illustrate the order of operations of a program.

intrinsic - a function (usually complex) which is built into the ROM.

K - kilo. Used to denote one thousand. 4K means four thousand.

load - to enter data into storage.

loop - a sequence of instructions which are repeated a specified number of times.

machine language - a code consisting of binary numbers which is directly understood by the computer.

program - a series of instructions to be performed by the computer.

RAM - the section of memory where information is temporarily stored.

ROM - the section of memory where information is permanently stored.

software - programs associated with a computer.

stochastic - a program which contains the element of randomality.

subroutine - a series of instructions, which may be looped, executed by a branch.

syntax - the rules governing the expression of statements and commands in a computer language.

variable - a quantity that is assigned a value, or set of values.

volatile memory - any memory which loses the data stored in it when the power to the computer is discontinued.

Index